THE
CRYPTO
DICTIONARY

bitcoinbasix.com

Published by Bitcoin Basix
Production and design by Bitcoin Basix
Edited by Tilo Grieco & Barry Radice

www.bitcoinbasix.com

All efforts have been made to ensure information is correct at time of printing. We welcome any information that rectifies inaccuracies or missing elements. Please send information to support@bitcoinbasix.com.

Copyright © 2018 Bitcoin Basix

All rights reserved. Without limiting the rights under the copyright above, no part of this publication may be reproduced, stored in or introduced into a retrieval system, or transmitted in any form or by any means (electronic, mechanical, photocopying, recording or otherwise), without the prior written permission of both the copyright owner and the publisher.

Disclaimer: Every attempt has been made to trace and acknowledge copyright. This has not been possible in all cases. Bitcoin Basix apologises for any accidental infringement and welcomes information that would recitfy this situation.

While every care has been taken to ensure the accuracy of the material presented, Bitcoin Basix, its partners, employees, or any of its representatives will not bear any responsibility or liability for action taken by any person on the basis of the information contained in this book. The content is for information purposes only. It is recommended that no person make an investment decision until such time as their individual needs, desires and risk profile have been assessed by a qualified professional.

CONTENTS

7 - Introduction

9 - ACRONYMS

15 - GLOSSARY
A-Z of crypto words, slang and terms.

51 - EXPOSITION
52 - ALTCOINS
54 - ASSET OR CURRENCY?
56 - BITCOIN
58 - BLOCKCHAIN
60 - DAO
62 - DAPP
64 - DECENTRALISATION
66 - DISTRIBUTED LEDGER
68 - DOUBLE SPENDING
70 - ETHEREUM
72 - FORKS
74 - ICO
76 - MINING
78 - OPPORTUNITIES
80 - PEER-TO-PEER
82 - PRIVACY COINS
84 - PROOF-OF-STAKE
86 - PROOF-OF-WORK
88 - SMART CONTRACTS
90 - STABLE COINS
92 - TRUST
94 - USING CRYPTO
96 - WALLETS

INTRODUCTION

Welcome to the first edition of The Crypto Dictionary.

We hope that this book can help you understand the fundamentals of Cryptocurrency, Blockchain, and trading. We want it to be an easy reference for noobs, minnows, whales or sharks. At whatever point you are at in your crypto journey we hope you find this information useful, demystifying and compelling.

This book is divided into three sections:

Acronyms: An easy to follow reference to meanings of the main abbreviations used in crypto conversations and the world of general trading.

Glossary: Explanations for the key words, terms, and slang used in the world of crypto and general trading.

Exposition: Taking a closer look at some of the main topics that help piece together the fundamentals of Cryptocurrency and the technology that makes it possible.

ACRONYMS

Acronyms have become part of the Crypto vernacular. Here's an easy reference to help you navigate the conversation.

2FA (TFA)	Two Factor Authentication
ANN	Annoucement
AAL	Account Abstract Layer
AC	Alternate Currency
ADC	Association of Digital Currency
AML	Anti-Money Laundering
AON	All-or-None
API	Application Programming Interface
ASIC	Application Specific Integrated Circuit
ATH	All Time High
ATL	All Time Low
BCN	Blockchain Consensus Network
BFT	Byzantine Fault Tolerance
BIOT	Blockchain Internet of Things
BIP	Bitcoin Improvement Proposal
BPI	Bitcoin Price Index
BTC	Bitcoin
BTD	Buy The Dip
BTFD	Buy The F$%king Dip
BU	Bitcoin Unlimited
C&H	Cup and Handle
cBTC	centiBitcoin (0.01)
CFTC	The U.S. "Commodity Futures Trading Commission
CYA	Cover your Ass
CYOA	Cover Your Own Ass
daBTC	decaBitcoin (10 BTC)
DAICO	Decentralized Autonomous ICO
DAO	Decentralized Autonomous Organizations
DAPPs	Decentralized Applications
dBTC	deciBitcoin (0.1 BTC)
DCA	Dollar Cost Averaging

DDoS	Distributed Denial of Service
DEX	Decentralized Exchange
DPoS	Delegated-Proof-of-Stake
DYOR	Do Your Own Research
EEA	Enterprise Ethereum Alliance
EIP	Ethereum Improvement Proposal
ELI5	Explain Like I'm 5
EMA	Exponential Moving Average
ERC	Ethereum Request for Comments
ERC-20	Ethereum Request for Comment (Request number:20)
ETF	Exchange Traded Fund
ETH	Ethereum
EVM	Ethereum Virtual Machine
EW	Elliot Wave
FA	Fundamental Analysis
FAQ	Frequently Asked Questions
FATCA	Foreign Account Tax Compliance Act
FBA	Federated Byzantine Agreement
Flash P&D	Flash Pump and dump
FOMO	Fear of missing out
FreeCO	Free Coin Offering
FUD	Fear, Uncertainty and Doubt
FUDster	Someone spreading FUD
GPU	Graphics Processing Unit
H&S	Head and shoulders
HF	Hard fork
HNWI	High-Net-Worth Individual
HODL	Hold
ICO	Initial Coin Offering
IMO	In My Opinion
IOC	Immediate-or-Cancel

IPFS	InterPlanetary File System
ISO	Initial Scam Offering
JOMO	Joy Of Missing Out
kBTC	kiloBitcoin (1,000 BTC)
KYC	Know Your Customer
Lambo	Lamborghini
LN	Lightning Network
MA	Moving Averages
MACD	Moving Average Convergence/Divergence Indicator
MASF	Miner Activated Soft Fork
MBTC	megaBitcoin (1,000,000 BTC)
mBTC	milliBitcoin (0.001 BTC)
MCAP	Market Capitalization
MEW	My Ethereum Wallet
MSB	Money Services Business
Multisig	Multisignature
MW	MimbleWimble
NADDIC	Never A Dull Day In Crypto
OCD	Obsessive Cryptocurrency Disorder
OCO	One Cancels the Other Order
OTC	Over The Counter
P&D (PND)	Pump and dump
P2P	Peer to Peer
PBFT	Practical Byzantine Fault Tolerance
PKI	Public Key Infrastructure
PoA	Proof-of-Authority
PoI	Proof-of-Importance
PoS	Proof-of-Stake
PoW	Proof-of-Work
QA	Qualitative Analysis
QR code	Quick Response Code

RBF	Replace-By-Fee
Rekt	Wrecked
RingCT	Ring Confidential Transactions
RNG	Random Number Generation
ROI	Return on Investment
RoRo	Risk On, Risk Off
RPOW	Reusable Proofs of Work
RSI	Relative Strength Index
SAFT	Simple Agreements for Future Tokens
SATS	Satoshi's
SEC	Securities and Exchange Commission (USA)
SegWit	Segregated witness
SF	Soft Fork
SHA	Secure Hash Algorithm
SoV	Store of Value
SPV	Simple Payment Verification
STO	Security Token Offering
TA	Technical Analysis
TGE	Token Generation Event
TOR	Terms of Reference
TPS	Transactions Per Second
TTD	Time To Dump
TWAP	Time-weighted average price
U2F	Universal 2-Factor
UAHF	User Activated Hard Fork
UASF	User Activated Soft Fork
uBTC	microBitcoin (0.000001)
UTXO	Unspent Transaction Output
VaR	Value at Risk
VC	Venture Capitalist
WTC	Welcome to Crypto

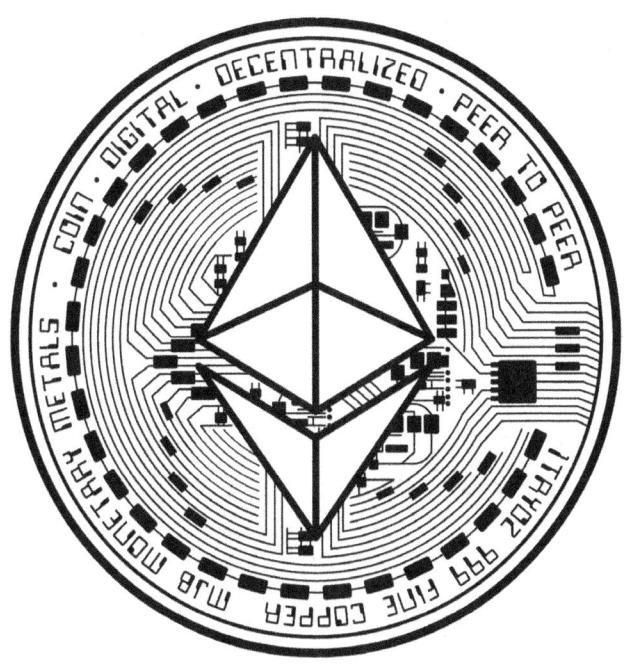

GLOSSARY

The A to Z of Crypto words, terms and slang.

2-FACTOR AUTHENTICATION
The process where a user must input a code from their phone to complete the signing in process.

51% ATTACK
Is a potential attack on a blockchain by a group of miners who control more than 50% of the network's mining hash rate, or computing power.

A

ACCOUNT ABSTRACT LAYER
Serves as a point of contact between the Bitcoin protocol and Ethereum Virtual Machine.

ADDRESSES
A unique identifier consisting of 26-35 alphanumeric characters. Addresses are used to send and receive cryptocurrencies.

AES HARDWARE ENCRYPTION
AES (Advance Encryption Standard). The international standard for data encryption/decryption.

AIRDROP
The free distribution of small amounts of digital currency tokens to members of its community usually for promotional purposes.

ALGORITHM
A set of rules outlined for specific problem-solving calculations.

ALL-TIME HIGH (ATH)
Buying pressure pushes the price of an asset up to highs it has never seen before.

ALL-TIME LOW (ATL)
Selling pressure pushes the price of an asset down to lows it has never seen before.

ALT SEASON
When many altcoins in the crypto market go to the 'moon'.

ALTCOIN
The combination of two words Alt and Coin. They represent alternative cryptocurrencies launched after the success of Bitcoin.

ANTI-MONEY LAUNDERING (AML)
Process that financial

institutions such as exchanges follow to prevent, detect and report money laundering activities.

APPLICATION PROGRAMMING INTERFACE (API)
Set of functions used by computer programs to request services from the operating system, software libraries or other services.

APPLICATION-SPECIFIC INTEGRATED CIRCUIT (ASIC)
An integrated circuit that has been customised for one specific task, rather than general purpose use.

ARBITRAGE
The simultaneous buying and selling of an asset to profit from the imbalance in the price across two different markets.

ASHDRAKED
Completely blow up your trading account by shorting Bitcoin.

ASIC MINER
Miners who use the SHA-256 hash algorithm.

ASK PRICE
The lowest price a seller of an asset is willing to accept for an asset.

ASYMMETRIC KEY ALGORITHMS
Also known as Asymmetric Cryptography. A branch of cryptography where a secret key can be divided into two parts. A public key and a private key.

ATOMIC SWAP
Smart contract technology which enables the exchange of one cryptocurrency for another without the need of centralized authorities.

ATTACK SURFACE
Vulnerable areas in a computing device or network that are accessible to hackers.

ATTESTATION LEDGER
An account book designed to provide evidence of individual transactions.

BAG
A stock that has decreased in value so much it has become worthless.

BAG HOLDER
An investor who holds an asset that has decreased so much, it has become worthless.

BART
A crypto chart pattern that resembles Bart Simpson's hair.

BEAR TRAP
A trap in which institutional investors appear to be shorting an asset but then suddenly change and start buying after stop losses have been taken out.

BEAR MARKET
When the market is lacking confidence and prices have dropped more than 20%.

BEAR TREND
A trend in the market where price is heading south.

BEARISH
If an investor is bearish, he or she is in the mindset of selling assets.

BEARWHALE
Someone who places a large sell order.

BID PRICE
The amount of money a buyer is willing to pay for an assest or security.

BID-ASK SPREAD
The amount the ask price exceeds the bid price.

BIG BLOCKERS
People who are in favour of increasing the block size.

BIP 148
A user-activated soft fork, which requires bitcoin miners to signal for SegWit.

BIT
A binary digit. The smallest unit of data, 0 or 1.

BIT GOLD
A proposal by Nick Szabo describing a system for the decentralised creation of unforgeable proof-of-work.

BITCOIN
A form of electronic currency used to purchase goods or services pseudononymously, using cryptography to verify transactions.

bitcoin (lowercase b)
The collection of technologies used by the bitcoin ledger.

Bitcoin (uppercase B)
The cryptocurrency.

BITCOIN CORE
Also known as the Satoshi client, Bitcoin Core is an open source project which maintains and releases Bitcoin client software.

BITCOIN IMPROVEMENT PROPOSAL
A document that has been designed to introduce features or information to Bitcoin.

BITCOIN INDEX
Monitoring all Bitcoin price movements, the Bitcoin Index relays the value of a single Bitcoin compared to fiat currencies.

BITCOIN MAXIMALISTS
People who favour bitcoin over other cryptocurrencies.

BITCOIN NETWORK
A peer-to-peer payment network that operates on a cryptographic protocol.

BITPAY
Payment-processing platform, which allows merchants to accept Bitcoin as payment.

BLACK SWAN
An event or occurrence that deviates beyond what is normally expected of a situation and is extremely difficult to predict.

BLOCK CONFIRMATION
The confirmation that a block has been added to the blockchain.

BLOCK EXPLORER
An online blockchain explorer that shows the contents of each block and transaction.

BLOCK HEIGHT
The number of blocks in a blockchain between itself and the genesis block. The genesis block has a height of 0.

BLOCK REWARD
The number of cryptocurrencies that are released by the blockchain to miners after they mine a block.

BLOCK TIMESTAMP
A record of when a transaction was processed.

BLOCKCHAIN
A digital, decentralised ledger of 'blocks' which are linked and verified using cryptography.

BLOCKCHAIN ASSET
A type of digital asset or cryptocurrency and sometimes represent stakes in a particular project or company.

BLOCKS
Blocks contain transaction data and are permanently recorded on a blockchain.

BLOODBATH
A period where major cryptocurrency prices tanked.

BOLLINGER BANDS
A type of statistical chart that characterises the prices and volatility over time.

BORROWING RATE
The amount charged by the lender to a borrower for the use of assets.

BOTS
A software application that runs automated tasks over the Internet.

BOUNTY
A job, task, or project created by coin developers. Complete the mission and receive a reward.

BTC
Ticker symbol used to represent bitcoin.

BUBBLE
A speculative bubble or mania where the price of an asset strongly exceeds its intrinsic value.

BUG BOUNTY
A deal offered by many websites and software developers where individuals receive recognition and compensation for reporting bugs in applications.

BULL MARKET
When the market is showing confidence. Indicators of confidence are prices going up.

BULL TRAP

A false signal indicating that a declining trend in a stock or asset has reversed and is heading upwards when in actual fact it will continue to head lower.

BULL TREND

A period of time where the price of an asset will head higher.

BULLISH

An asset that is being aggressively bought is considered as bullish.

BURNED

A method of burning cryptocurrencies to increase the value of the remaining cryptocurrencies.

BUTTHURT

An excessive or unjustifiable feeling of personal offence.

BUY THE FU**IN DIP (BTFD)

Refers to the method of buying an asset during a decline in price.

BUY WALL

A wall of buy orders considerably higher than the sell orders.

BYZANTINE FAULT TOLERANCE

The dependability of a fault-tolerant computer system, particularly distributed computing systems.

CANDLESTICKS

The popular chart representation of the live price of an asset. In the shape of a candlestick, the chart illuminates the highest and lowest trades for the day.

CAPITAL CONTROL

Any measure taken by governments or regulatory bodies limiting the flow of foreign capital in and out of a domestic economy.

CENTRAL LEDGER

A central repository that stores records of transactions.

CHAIN LINKING

A proposition to connect smart contracts across blockchain by allowing smart contracts to access key off-chain resources.

CHARGEBACK
Transaction reversal made to dispute a card transaction and secure a refund for the purchase.

CHECKPOINT LOCKIN
When an old block hash is hard coded into Bitcoin software as optimization for the initial blockchain download.

CIPHER
A way to encode information to make it unreadable. An algorithm that performs encryption or decryption.

CIRCULATING SUPPLY
The number of cryptocurrencies in circulation in the market.

CLIENT
In computing, a client is a desktop or workstation that is capable of obtaining information and applications from a server.

COINBASE TRANSACTION
Transaction inside a block that pays the miner a block reward.

COLD WALLET
Sometimes referred to as an offline wallet where you store your cryptocurrencies offline.

COMMODITY MONEY
Money whose value comes from a commodity of which it is made, such as gold.

CONFIRMATION
Relating to either technical indicators or fundamental data that confirms a hypothesis thereby allowing you to enter a trade.

CONFIRMED
If a transaction has been confirmed, it means that it cannot be reversed.

CONFLUENCE
The combination of multiple strategies and ideas into one complete strategy.

CONSENSUS
A general agreement that is followed. For example, when a fork takes place, a consensus is reached to initiate it.

CONSENSUS MECHANISM
A fault-tolerant mechanism used to achieve a consensus on a single data value or a single state of the network.

CONSENSUS POINT
A point which is the result of technical analysis being carried out.

CONSENSUS PROCESS
A group decision-making process, where all members agree to support a decision.

CONSENSUS RULE
A rule where a decision cannot be made unless all participating parties are in agreement.

CONSORTIUM BLOCKCHAIN
A blockchain that is semi-privately owned rather than a public platform such as the Bitcoin Blockchain.

CONTAGION
Market movement that spreads from one market to another.

CONTENTIOUS HARD FORK
Disagreements in a community sometimes results in a group creating a new chain by introducing major changes to the code.

CONTRACT
I.e. Future Contract which are forward contracts between a buyer and seller of an asset. They agree to exchange goods and money at a future date.

CONTRACT BYTE CODE
A contract with specific instructions that are executed by a software program.

CORRECTION
A rapid change in the nominal price of a commodity.

COUNTERPARTY RISK
Risk to each party of a contract that counterparty will not live up to its contractual obligations.

COVER YOUR ASS/ COVER YOUR OWN ASS
A method of covering one's back in the event of something happening.

CROSS-BORDER TRANSACTION
A transaction that occurs internationally.

CROWDSALE
A new way to use cryptocurrency technology to issue tokens that represent shares or equity.

CROWDSOURCING
A way of raising money by appealing to crowds of people, which also limits the risk on each investor.

CRYPTO
Abreviation for cryptocurrency or cryptocurrencies.

CRYPTO VAULT
Next level cold storage. A physical vault which removes the risk of losing your recovery seed or losing your USB cold storage.

CRYPTO-ANARCHIST
Anarchists who use cryptographic means to work towards building their ideal society.

CRYPTOANALYSIS
The method of analysing multiple cryptocurrencies.

CRYPTOCURRENCY
A form of virtual currency that relies upon cryptography for security.

CRYPTOGRAPHIC HASH
A function that takes input and returns a fixed-size alphanumeric string, which is called the 'hash value.'

CRYPTOGRAPHIC HASH FUNCTION
A special class of hash function that has certain properties which make it suitable for use in cryptography.

CRYPTOGRAPHY
Used to create codes that allow information to be kept secret. It turns readable data into unreadable data.

CRYPTOJACKING
A form of cyber attack where a hacker secretly uses your computer to mine cryptocurrency.

CRYPTOPHOBIA
A fear or mistrust of Cryptocurrency.

CUP AND HANDLE
A candle chart formation that makes out the shape of a cup and handle. Identifies resistance.

CYPHERPUNK
Any activist advocating widespread use of strong cryptography and privacy-enhancing technologies.

D

DAICO
A way to make ICOs more secure by involving investors in the initial project development process.

DAO
A digital autonomous organisation that is run through rules that are encoded as smart contracts.

DAPP
A decentralised application that is run by many users on a decentralised network with trustless protocols.

DARKNET
Networks that are not indexed by search engines such as Google, Yahoo or Bing. These networks aren't available to the general Internet public.

DATA MINING
Sorting through large data sets in order to identify patterns and establish relationships to solve problems through data analysis.

DAY TRADE
Buy and sell within 24 hours.

DEAD CAT BOUNCE
A small and temporary recovery in a financial market following a large fall.

DECENTRALISATION
A way of removing authority from a central authority.

DECENTRALISED EXCHANGE
Exchange platform that doesn't rely on third-party services to hold customers funds.

DECRYPTION
The process of taking encoded or encrypted text or data and converting it back into a format that can be read.

DEFLATION
The process of reducing the general level of prices in an economy.

DELEGATED PROOF-OF-STAKE
Allows the owner of a cryptocurrency to vote for a delegate to perform the function of validating transactions and maintaining the blockchain.

DENIAL-OF-SERVICE ATTACK
A cyber attack where the perpetrator seeks to make a machine or network resource unavailable to its intended users by disrupting service of a host connected to the internet.

DEPTH
The market's ability to sustain relatively large market orders without impacting the price of the asset.

DEPTH CHART
A chart to show the market depth of a particular asset.

DESKTOP WALLET
A wallet that you keep on your desktop to store your cryptocurrencies.

DETERMINISTIC WALLET
A system of deriving keys from a single starting point known as a seed.

DIGITAL ASSET
An electronic asset that resides solely in the realm of computers.

DIGITAL CERTIFICATE
Used with self-signatures and message encryption, and are issued by a certification authority.

DIGITAL COMMODITY
A tradable commodity that has value and is digital, such as cryptocurrencies.

DIGITAL IDENTITY
The network or Internet equivalent to the identity of a real person or entity.

DIGITAL SIGNATURE
A mathematical scheme for demonstrating the authenticity of digital messages or documents.

DISTRIBUTED DENIAL OF SERVICE
An attack in which multiple compromised computer systems attack a target, such as a server.

DISTRIBUTED LEDGER
A database that is constantly updated independently by each participant on a large network.

DIVERSIFICATION
A risk management strategy that mixes a variety of investment within a portfolio.

DO YOUR OWN RESEARCH (DYOR)
Stop asking people which coins to buy - DYOR.

DOLLAR COST AVERAGING
An investment strategy with the goal of reducing the impact of volatility on large purchases of financial assets. Fixed amount purchases are scheduled regardless of share price.

DOLPHINS
Investors with significant holdings.

DOUBLE SPENDING
A flaw in electronic cash schemes in which one single digital token can be spent more than once.

DUMP
Where institutional investors will sell an asset after a pump.

DUMPING
Selling an asset after a period of strong buying power.

DUST TRANSACTION
A transaction that has a value lower than the minimum limit of a valid transaction.

E

ELLIOTT WAVE
A form of technical analysis that traders use to analyse financial market cycles and forecast market trends.

ENCRYPTION
Process of encoding a message or information in a way that only authorized parties can access it.

ENTERPRISE ETHEREUM ALLIANCE (EEA)
Alliance built to customise ethereum by defining enterprise-grade software that is capable of complex, high demand applications.

EQUITY TOKENS
Tokens that represent equity in a company through the use of Ethereum-based smart contracts.

ERC-20
A technical standard used for smart contracts on the Ethereum blockchain for implementing tokens. ERC stands for Ethereum Request for Comment.

ESCROW
A contractual agreement in which a third party receives and disburses money or documents for the primary transacting parties.

ETHER
The underlying token powering the Ethereum blockchain.

ETHEREUM
A decentralised platform for applications that run exactly as programmed without any chance of fraud, censorship or third-party interference.

ETHEREUM IMPROVEMENT PROPOSAL
Describe the standards for the Ethereum platform, including core protocol specifications, client APIs, and contract standards.

ETHEREUM VIRTUAL MACHINE
Focuses on providing security and executing untrusted code by computers all over the world.

EXCHANGE
A marketplace to buy, sell and trade different cryptocurrencies.

EXCHANGE TRADED FUND (ETF)
A type of investment fund that is traded on a stock exchange but tracks an index or securities.

EXPLAIN LIKE I'M 5 (ELI5)
The concept of breaking something down to explain to someone in simple terms.

EXPONENTIAL MOVING AVERAGE (EMA)
A moving average that places a greater weight and significance on the most recent data points.

F

FAKE WALL
When whales place large orders that mimic other buy/sell orders.

FAUCET
A rewards system, drip feeding small amounts of coins or tokens in return for tasks completed or promotional activity.

FEAR, UNCERTAINTY AND DOUBT (FUD)
A marketing strategy used

to cast a shadow over other cryptocurrencies perpetuating emotions felt in times of panic or unrest.

FEDERATED BYZANTINE AGREEMENT
Method get a consensus on a blockchain network. In FBA systems, each node does not have to be known and verified ahead of time, membership is open and control is decentralised.

FIAT
Traditional currency declared as legal tender by a government but is not backed by a physical commodity like gold.

FIATSPLAINING
Someone with a traditional finance background trying to explain how cryptocurrency works.

FIBONACCI RETRACEMENTS
Ratios based on the Fibonacci sequence, used to identify potential reversal levels.

FIBONACCI SEQUENCE
A series of numbers found by adding up the two numbers before it.

FILL OR KILL
A type of equity order that requires immediate and complete execution of a trade or its cancellation.

FLASH PUMP AND DUMP
Pump and dump that happens faster than usual. A period of buying pressure and then a serious spell of selling occurs.

FLIP
To buy a crypto asset, usually via an ICO, and then quickly sell it for a profit.

FOMO
Fear Of Missing Out.

FOREIGN ACCOUNT TAX COMPLIANCE ACT
A law that requires foreign financial institutions and certain other non-financial foreign entities to report on their foreign assets held by their U.S. account holders.

FORGING
The creation of new blocks in blockchain based on the Proof-of-Stake algorithm.

FORK
When a Blockchain is split into two.

FREEZING OF ASSETS
Legal prevention of the dissipating assets from beyond the jurisdiction of a court.

FRONTIER
The first release of Ethereum named Frontier.

FUDSTER
Someone spreading Fear, Uncertainty and Doubt.

FULL NODE
A program that fully validates transactions and blocks.

FUNDAMENTAL ANALYSIS
The process of conducting analysis based on economic data.

FUNGIBLE
An asset can be fungible if it is replaceable by another identical asset.

FUTURES CONTRACT
A forward-looking contract for assets bought at an agreed price but delivered and paid for later.

G

GAS
Used to conduct a transaction or execute a contract on the Ethereum blockchain.

GAS LIMIT
The amount of fuel required to execute an operation or run a particular smart contract.

GAS PRICE
The internal pricing for running a transaction or contract on the Ethereum blockchain.

GENESIS BLOCK
The genesis block is the first block in a blockchain.

GRAPHICS PROCESSING UNIT (GPU)
A specialised unit designed to rapidly manipulate and alter memory to accelerate the creation of images.

GWEI
A denomination of Ether.

H

HALVING
When miners rewards are reduced by 50%.

HARD CAP
The maximum amount of money a cryptocurrency can receive from investors in its initial coin offering.

HARD FORK
When a single cryptocurrency splits into two. This refers to a radical change to the protocol that makes previously invalid blocks/transactions valid.

HARDWARE WALLET
A physical device that is used to store your cryptocurrencies or tokens.

HASH
A function which converts a data input into an alphanumeric string.

HASH ALGORITHM
A cryptographic hash function that maps data or arbitrary size to a hash of a fixed size.

HASHCASH
A proof-of-work system used to limit email spam and denial-of-service attacks.

HASHING POWER
The amount of power a computer uses to solve hashing algorithms.

HASHRATE
The measuring unit of the processing power of a proof-of-work based cryptocurrency network.

HD WALLET
Short for Hierarchical Deterministic wallet, they all use 12-word master seed keys.

HEAD AND SHOULDERS
Technical charting pattern where charts resemble a head and two shoulders. Good for identifying support and resistance.

HIGH-NET-WORTH INDIVIDUAL (HNWI)
A term used to describe someone whose investable assets are higher than the average.

HODL
Slang term used when referring to holding a cryptocurrency rather than selling it.

HOLD
Holding onto a position for an extended period of time.

HOMESTEAD
The second major release of the Ethereum platform.

HOT WALLET
A wallet that is connected to the Internet.

HYPERBITCOINIZATION
When bitcoin's rising value causes a rush from fiat currencies to crypto.

ICEBERG ORDER
Orders on public exchanges that are only partially visible.

IMMEDIATE OR CANCEL
Requires all or part of the order to be executed immediately and unfilled parts of the order cancelled.

INITIAL COIN OFFERING (ICO)
The process of raising funds in exchange for coins or tokens.

INITIAL SCAM OFFERING
Scams that masquerade themselves as legitimate initial coin offerings.

INPUT
Information or data sent to a computer for processing.

INTERMEDIARY
A person who acts as a link between people in order to bring about an agreement.

INTEROPERABILITY
The ability of computer systems or software to exchange and make use of information.

INTERPLANETARY FILE SYSTEM (IPFS)
A permanent and decentralised method of storing and sharing files.

IRREVERSIBLE
Unable to reverse a transaction once it has taken place.

J, K, L

JOY OF MISSING OUT
The opposite of FOMO, where someone is happy to have missed out on opportunities.

KNOW YOUR CUSTOMER (KYC)
The process of a business

verifying the identity of its clients.

LADDERING
An investment technique that involves purchasing multiple financial products with different maturity dates.

LAMBO
Short for Lamborghini.

LEDGER
The principal book or computer file for recording and totaling economic transactions.

LEVERAGE
The use of various financial instruments or borrowed capital to increase the potential return of an investment.

LIGHT NODE
A light node only downloads the blockheaders instead of the complete blockchain making easier to maintain and run.

LIGHTNING NETWORK
A second layer peer-to-peer system for making micropayments of digital currencies.

LIMIT ORDER
A buy or sell order set at a specific price.

LIQUIDITY
The degree to which an asset can be quickly bought or sold.

LOCK TIME
Part of a transaction which indicates the earliest time or earliest block when that transaction may be added to the blockchain.

LONG
The act of buying an asset with the intention of selling it at a higher price.

LONG TERM HOLD
The act of holding a position for a long time.

M OF N CONTROL POLICY
Back-up process of public and private key material over multiple systems or devices.

MAIN CHAIN
The linear chain to which all other chains, long or short or both, are dependant.

MAINNET
The original and main network for bitcoin transactions, where satoshis have real economic value.

MAKER FEE/TAKER FEE
Fees or commissions used to stimulate market activity.

MARGIN BEAR POSITION
The inverse of a bull position. A bear position is a bet against the price of a trade or investment rising or staying flat.

MARGIN BULL POSITION
Is a long position in a security where the trader looks to profit from rising prices.

MARGIN CALL
When a broker demands additional money in order to cover possible losses.

MARGIN TRADING
The practice of using borrowed funds from a broker to trade a financial asset.

MARKET CAPITALISATION (CAP)
The total market value of a cryptocurrency.

MARKET MAKERS
A dealer in securities or other assets who undertakes to buy or sell at specified prices at all times.

MARKET ORDER
A buy or sell order to be executed immediately at current market prices.

MARKET SENTIMENT
The overall attitude of investors towards a particular asset or market.

MASTERNODE
A node or computer that keeps the full copy of the blockchain in real-time.

MAXIMUM SUPPLY
The total amount of cryptocurrency that will be available to mine.

mBTC
1 thousandth of a Bitcoin (0.001 BTC).

MEDIUM OF EXCHANGE
An intermediary instrument used to facilitate the sale, purchase or trade of goods.

MEDIUM TERM HOLD
A period of time normally

extending from a few weeks to a few months where a trader holds a trade.

MEMPOOL
Short for memory pool. When a transaction has been conducted over a network it is transmitted and held in what is known as a mempool.

MERKLE ROOT
A merkle root contains all the information about every transaction hash that exists on a block.

MERKLE TREE
Also known as a hash tree is a tree in which every leaf node is labeled with the has of a data block.

METROPOLIS
The third major release of the Ethereum platform.

MEW
Short for MyEtherWallet.

MICROTRANSACTION
Often abbreviated to MTX where users can transfer amounts as low as 5 cents. Impossible with the current system as it would incur prohibitive transaction fees.

MIMBLEWIMBLE
A proposal for a bitcoin-like blockchain that could be implemented as a side chain.

MINER ACTIVATED SOFT FORK
A mechanism by which miners trigger the activation of soft forks when a majority signals the readiness to upgrade.

MINERS
People who verify and add transactions to the blockchain digital ledger in exchange for a reward based in cryptocurrency.

MINING
A process where transactions for cryptocurrencies are verified and added to the blockchain.

MINING ALGORITHM
A program that is used to mine cryptocurrencies, such as the SHA-256 algorithm.

MINING DIFFICULTY
The time it takes to find a new block and place it in the blockchain.

MINING POOL
The act of pooling resources together by miners who share processing power over a network.

MINING POOL REWARD
The reward a miner gets for successfully placing a new block into the blockchain.

MINING POOL REWARD - CAPPED PAY PER SHARE WITH RECENT BACKPAY (CPPSRB)
A mining pool will pay as many shares as it can every time a block is found.

MINING POOL REWARD - PAY PER LAST N SHARE (PPLN)
Payment to miners in the form of a percentage of shares they contribute to the total shares.

MINING POOL REWARD - PAY PER SHARE (PPS)
Payments are paid to miners based on the number of shares they own.

MINING POOL REWARD - PROP
When a block is found, the reward is shared proportionally amongst all worker based on how many shares they found.

MINING POOL REWARD - THE DOUBLE GEOMETRIC METHOD (DGM)
The operator receives a portion of payout on short rounds and returns it on longer rounds to normalize payments.

MINING RIG
A physical structure that contains different components used to mine cryptocurrencies.

MINNOW
A slang term used to describe newbies in the cryptocurrency space.

MIXING SERVICE
A service offered to mix potentially identifiable or tainted cryptocurrency funds with others.

MOBILE WALLET
A wallet that is kept on a users mobile device.

MONEY SERVICES BUSINESS
A legal term used by financial regulators to describe a

business that transmits or convert money.

MOON
Used to express the joy and elation when an altcoin is pumped by a whale, giving the illusion that they have invested intelligently.

MOONING
Refers to the price of a cryptocurrency rising exponentially.

MOVING AVERAGE CONVERGENCE DIVERGENCE (MACD)
A trend-following momentum indicator used to show the relationship between moving averages.

MULTIPOOL
The process of jumping across from crypto to crypto and mining the most profitable.

MULTISIGNATURE
A digital signature scheme which allows a group of users to sign a single document.

N

NATSPEC
Originally developed for annotating code for automatic documentation generation.

NETWORK
A global connection of nodes or computers that operate on a blockchain that monitor and maintain the network.

NOCOINER
Someone who has no Cryptocurrency.

NODES
Computers on a blockchain network that maintain it.

NONCE
An arbitrary number that can be used just once.

NOOB
A person who is new to crypto.

O

OBSESSIVE CRYPTOCURRENCY DISORDER
Someone who is obsessed with cryptocurrencies.

OFF-LEDGER CURRENCY
All currencies that can be used with but weren't created for a specific digital wallet.

OFFLINE STORAGE
A place that is not connected to the Internet where you can keep your cryptocurrencies.

ONE CANCELS THE OTHER ORDER
A pair of orders stipulating that is one order executes, then the other order is automatically canceled.

OPEN-SOURCE SOFTWARE
Software with accessible source code that people can modify and share.

ORACLES
An agent that finds and verifies real-world occurrences and submits this information to a blockchain to be used by smart contracts.

ORDER BOOK
An electronic list of buy and sell orders for a specific security or financial instrument organised by price level.

ORPHAN BLOCKS
Blocks received by a node but does not have its entire ancestry and cannot be validated.

OUTPUT
An output of a blockchain transaction that has not been spent.

OVER THE COUNTER (OTC)
Assets that are traded through a dealer network such as an online trading platform.

OVERBOUGHT
Referring to an asset that traders believe is trading above its true value.

OVERSOLD
Sold at a price that is believed to be below its true value.

PANIC
An emotional state in financial markets where participants tend to sell more than they buy.

PAPER WALLET
A wallet where your public and private keys are kept on a piece of paper.

PAYMENT PROCESSORS
A company appointed by a merchant to handle transactions from various channels such as credit cards and debit cards.

PEER-TO-PEER
Computer systems which are connected to each other via the internet, accessing files without the need for a central server.

PEER-TO-PEER EXCHANGE
Decentralised buying and selling of assets such as cryptocurrencies online.

PERMISSIONED BLOCKCHAIN
Users need to approval before they can start mining.

PERMISSIONLESS
A permissionless blockchain is an open ecosystem in which any user is able to join the network and start mining to help validate transactions.

PONZI SCHEME
A form of fraud where someone lures investors and pays profits to early investors using the funds obtained from newer investors.

POOL
A group of investors that 'pool' their money together in order to achieve greater buying power. Also a goup of miners working together to mine and share rewards for cryptocurrencies.

POOL REWARD
The reward given to the pool of miners after a successful crypto mining operation.

POST-ONLY ORDER
An order that doesn't remove liquidity from the system upon entry.

PRACTICAL BYZANTINE FAULT TOLERANCE
Meaning two nodes can communicate safely across a network, knowing that they are displaying the same data.

PRE-SALE
A period of time where an asset is available for purchase to a select group of before before the actual sale.

PRIVATE KEY
A large numerical value used to decrypt the data in the corresponding public key.

PRIVATESEND
A decentralised coin mixer feature on the Dash protocol that is designed to enhance user financial privacy.

PROOF-OF-AUTHORITY
An algorithm used with blockchains that delivers comparatively fast transactions through a consensus mechanism.

PROOF-OF-IMPORTANCE
A blockchain algorithm similar to proof-of-authority that was introduced by NEM, where nodes need to 'vest' an amount of currency to be eligible for creating blocks and are selected for creating a block roughly in proportion to some score.

PROOF-OF-STAKE
A consensus distribution algorithm that rewards earnings based on the number of coins that you own.

PROOF-OF-WORK
A consensus distribution algorithm that rewards those who put more 'work' in.

PROTOCOLS
Certain rules that blockchain networks are required to function properly and how to handle transactions.

PUBLIC ADDRESS
A form of identification and destination where cryptocurrencies can be sent.

PUBLIC BLOCKCHAIN
A public blockchain has absolutely no access restrictions.

PUBLIC KEY
A large numerical value used to encrypt data and to verify digital signatures linked to a private key.

PUBLIC KEY INFRASTRUCTURE
Actions required to manage digital certificates and public-key encryption.

PUMP
Artificially pumping asset prices up to give the impression that the asset is a worthy investment.

PUMP AND DUMP
The act of artificially inflating the price of an asset to attract buyers, only to then sell the asset.

PUMPING
The act of pumping the price of an asset up to attract buyers.

PUT OPTIONS
An option to sell assets at an agreed price on or before a particular date.

PYRAMID
Referring to a pyramid scheme that is similar to a Ponzi Scheme where new investment is used to pay older investments.

QUALITATIVE ANALYSIS
A securities analysis that uses subjective judgement based on unquantifiable information.

QUICK RESPONSE CODE
Known as a QR Code is the trademark for a type of matrix barcode.

RAIDEN NETWORK
An off-chain scaling solution that allows for near-instant, low-fee, and scalable payments.

RANDOM NUMBER GENERATION
The process of creating a random sequence of numbers.

RECIPIENT
A recipient receives something such as a payment.

REKT
Alternate spelling of 'wrecked'. The feeling you have after you've lost more than you should have.

RECOVERY PHRASE
A backup seed phrase is a list of words which allows access to your wallet if you forget your password. Also known as: Recovery seed, Seed Key, Recovery Key, Seed Phrase.

RELATIVE STRENGTH INDEX
Momentum indicator measuring the magnitude of recent price changes to analyse overbought or oversold conditions.

REMITTANCE
A sum of money sent as payment or as a gift.

REPLACE-BY-FEE
Allows a transaction to replace older ones so long as it pays a sufficient fee.

REPLICATED LEDGER
A copy of a distributed ledger in a network which is distributed to all participants in a network.

RESISTANCE
An area where the price of an asset struggles to break through.

RESISTANCE LEVEL
A level on a chart where price seems to struggle to break past.

RETURN ON INVESTMENT (ROI)
The amount of return you can expect to receive on your initial investment.

REUSABLE PROOF-OF-WORK (RPOW)
A prototype for a digital cash an early step in the history of digital cash.

REVERSE INDICATOR
Like the SAR indicator which stands for "stop and reverse" and trails price overtime.

RING CONFIDENTIAL TRANSACTIONS
A privacy feature implemented into the Monero protocol.

RING SIGNATURE
A digital signature that can be performed by any member of a group of users as long as each of them has keys.

S

SAJ CANDLE
A big green candle.

SATOSHI
Smallest unit of Bitcoin (0.00000001 BTC).

SATOSHI NAKAMOTO
Pseudonym used by the unknown person or people who developed bitcoin.

SCALABILITY
The capacity of a system, network or process to handle a growing amount of work.

SCAMCOIN
A coin which is only really profitable for the developers not for investors.

SCRYPT
An algorithm specifically designed to make it time consuming and financially prohibitive to perform large-scale custom hardware attacks.

SECURE HASH ALGORITHM
A cryptographic hash function which takes an input and produces a 160-bit hash value known as a message digest.

SEED NODES
The first nodes of the network.

SEED PHRASE
A secret list of words needed to recover a cryptocurrency wallet.

SEGWIT
Stands for Segregated Witness, which is a protocol upgrade that changes the way data is stored.

SEGWIT2X
Proposed hard fork of Bitcoin, but was called off due to a lack of support.

SELFISH MINING
A bitcoin mining strategy that maximises profits for miners at the cost of centralising the system by misleading fellow miners in the network.

SELL WALL
A tool used by rich individuals to manipulate the price of a cryptocurrency downwards.

SELLING PRESSURE
This occurs when the majority of the traders are selling, indicating that the majority think the market price will decrease.

SETTLEMENT SYSTEM
A process where securities or interests in securities are delivered, usually against payment of money to fulfill contractual obligations.

SHA 256
Secure Hash Algorithms-256 generates an almost-unique 256-bit (32-byte) signature.

SHAPESHIFT
A leading instant digital asset exchange platform that supports dozens of blockchain tokens.

SHARDING
A concept to make databases more scalable and efficient.

SHARKS
Investors with significant holding turn into sharks when they begin actively manipulating token prices.

SHILL
Someone endorsing a product as a consumer when they actually have a vested interest.

SHILLING
Creating hype or buzz surrounding a cryptocurrency to increase its value.

SHITCOIN
An altcoin that has become worthless.

SHORT
To short an asset on the financial markets means to sell.

SHORT TERM HOLD
The time period for a short term hold can be from a few hours to a few days.

SIDECHAIN
Emerging mechanisms that allow tokens and other digital assets from one blockchain to be securely used in a separate blockchain and then be moved back to the original blockchain if needed.

SIMPLE PAYMENT VERIFICATION (SPV)
Verification that a transaction is included in the Bitcoin blockchain without downloading the entire blockchain.

SLIPPAGE
Refers to the difference between the expected price of a trade and the price at which the trade is actually executed.

SMALL BLOCKERS
Small blockers see bitcoin failing when the individual is no longer able to operate a full node.

SMART CONTRACT
Programmable contracts that carry out specific functions.

SNIPER TRADES
Rrading strategy where a trader is selective with their trades being careful not to over trade.

SOFT CAP
The minimum amount of money a cryptocurrency can

receive from investors in its initial coin offering.

SOFT FORK
A change to the bitcoin protocol wherein only previously valid blocks/transactions are made invalid.

SOLIDITY
Ethereum's programming language for developing smart contracts.

SOLIDITY CONTRACT SOURCE CODE
A statically-typed curly-braces programming language designed for developing smart contracts that run on the Ethereum Virtual Machine.

SPOOFING
In programming, spoofing is where a person or program successfully masks itself as another by falsifying data.

STABLECOIN
A cryptocurrency that is pegged to a stable asset, such as gold or fiat.

STAKING
Is the mining of Proof-of-Stake coins.

STALE BLOCK
A block that is produced by building on an block that is no longer the active tip of the chain.

STATE CHANNEL
A way of moving blockchain interactions into high-speed, low-cost dedicated highways.

STEALTH ADDRESS
Additional security for the recipient of a digital currency by creating a random one-time address for a given transaction.

STOP LOSS
An order placed with a broker to sell a security when it reaches a certain price.

SUPERNODE
Any node that serves as one of the network's relayers and proxy servers.

SUPERCONDUCTING TRANSACTION
The ability for two users to exchange cryptocurrency from different blockchains in a completely trustless manner via a smart contract.

SUPPLY AND DEMAND
The balance between how in demand a product is in relation to its supply.

SUPPORT
A price level where a downtrend can be expected to pause due to a concentration of demand.

SWING
A short-term trading method that can be used when trading assets or securities. Swing trades typically last two to six days.

SYBIL ATTACK
An attack wherein a reputation system is subverted by forging identities in peer-to-peer networks.

TAKE-PROFIT ORDER
An order that closes the trade once it reaches a certain level of profit.

TECHNICAL ANALYSIS
The art of conducting analysis using technical indicators such as the MACD, or EMA.

TESTNET
Alternative Bitcoin block chain used for testing.

THE FLIPPENING
The point when Ethereum overtakes Bitcoin in market cap.

THIS IS GENTLEMEN
Originally a misspelling of This is it, gentlemen but now used to point out nice things.

TICKER SYMBOLS
Arrangement of characters that represent a particular security listed on an exchange.

TIME TO DUMP
The process where market leaders sell a pumped up security that other investors have bought into .

TIMESTAMP
A sequence of characters or encoded information identifying when a certain event occurred, usually giving a date and time.

TO THE MOON
A rise in price so astronomical it reaches the moon.

TOKENLESS LEDGER
Refers to a distributed ledger that doesn't require a type of currency to function.

TOKENS
Also known as cryptocurrencies, they are representations of digital assets.

TOTAL SUPPLY
Total amount of cryptocurrency available to mine.

TRADING BOT
Computer programs that use various indicators to recognise trends and automatically execute trades.

TRADING VOLUME
The total quantity of shares or contracts traded for a specified security.

TRANSACTION
An instance of buying or selling something.

TRANSACTION BLOCK
Where transaction data is permanently recorded in files called blocks.

TRANSACTION FEES
There are three main types of transaction fees in crypto: Fees for trading on an exchange, for transaction verification and Wallet fees.

TRANSACTION ID
An identification number for a cryptocurrency transaction.

TRANSACTIONS PER SECOND (TPS)
The number of transactions completed in one second by an information system.

TRUSTLESS
Referring to a blockchain which was designed so that nobody has to trust anybody else in order for the system to function.

TURING COMPLETE
If a computer can solve any problem that a turing machine can, then it is said to be turing complete.

TURING MACHINE
A mathematical model of a hypothetical computing machine which can be a predefined set of rules to determine a result from a set of input variables.

TWAP TRADES
Time-weighted average price trading is an algorithm based on weighted average price used to execute bigger orders without excessive impact on market price.

uBTC
A microbitcoin equal to 1 millionth of a Bitcoin represented as 0.000001BTC.

UNCONFIRMED TRANSACTION
A transaction that has not been included in a block and has not been completed.

UNSPENT TRANSACTION OUTPUT
An output of a blockchain transaction that has not been spent.

USER-ACTIVATED HARD FORK
A proposal to alter the Bitcoin protocol by creating a new fork in the Bitcoin software, which will operate on its own.

USER-ACTIVATED SOFT FORK
A mechanism where the activation time of a soft fork occurs on a specific date enforced by full nodes.

UTILITY
In economics, utility is used to model worth or value.

UTILITY TOKEN
Provide the owners with future access to a startup's services or products.

VANITY ADDRESS
An address where you are able to choose part of it yourself.

VENTURE CAPITALIST
Someone who invests in business ventures, providing capital for start-up or expansion.

VIRGIN BITCOIN
A Bitcoin received as a block reward which has never been spent before.

WALLETS
A place in which you can store your cryptocurrencies.

WEAK HANDS
Emotional trading that leads to selling early at the the sign of a drop.

WEI
The smallest denomination of ether. 1 Ether = 1,000,000,000,000,000,000 Wei.

WHALE
Investors that have a large impact on the market.

WHITE PAPER
An exhaustive report or guide that includes commercial, technological and financial details of a new coin in order to influence investors.

WHITELIST
A signup program that guarantees access to an ICO.

WIRE TRANSFER
An electronic transfer of money, where it goes from one bank to another.

WRECKED
Or rekt as in someone might get rekt. Usually referring to someone losing a lot of money.

YELLOW PAPER
A document that contains research that has not yet been formally accepted or published in an academic journal.

ZERO CONFIRMATION TRANSACTION
Where a transaction takes place but has not been confirmed on the blockchain.

ZERO KNOWLEDGE PROOF
A method where one party can prove to another party that they know a value of X, without conveying any information apart from the fact that she knows the value of X.

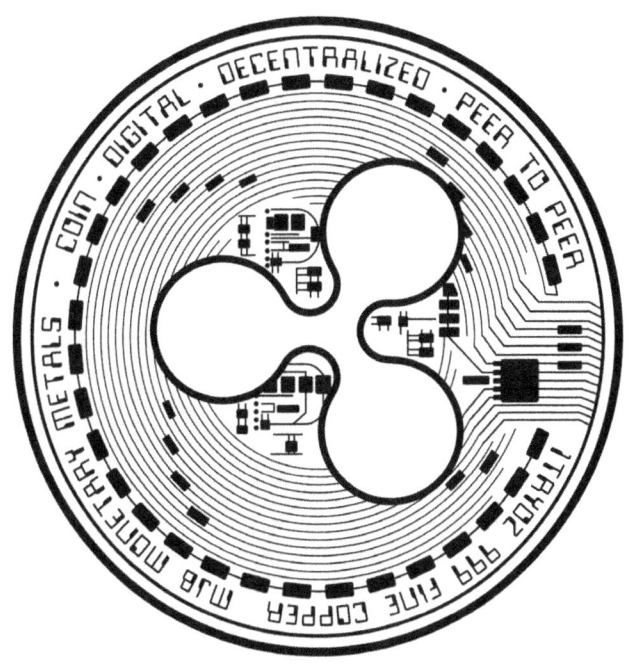

EXPOSITION

An in-depth look at key topics you need to understand about Cryptocurrency.

ALTCOINS

An altcoin is any digital cryptocurrency similar to Bitcoin. The term is said to stand for 'alternative to Bitcoin' and is used to describe any cryptocurrency that is not a Bitcoin.

Most popular altcoins use the same fundamental building blocks as Bitcoin. This approach is relatively easy to carry out because Bitcoin is a free, open-source platform.

When an altcoin forks at the blockchain level, an alternate system of consensus rules must be used, and the coin will have an entirely different distributed ledger. The same is true for altcoins built from scratch.

Some altcoins have different monetary policy rules built into the currency to encourage different uses and treatment. Policies such as minimum spend, or positive or negative interest on coins stored, can encourage or discourage hoarding.

Policies for coin mining may function differently from Bitcoin, as may the number of coins paid out per new block mined.

Some altcoins are made to discourage ASIC or GPU mining. This limitation is designed to reduce the advantage of specialised coin miners, as in the case of Litecoin, upon which half of all altcoins are based.

An altcoin blockchain may also store different metadata about the coin's previous transactions or may allow the coin to be repurposed as an alternate asset.

While some altcoins can be formed to enrich the founders and offer little new to the cryptocurrency marketplace, many have found niches because of the way their differences encouraged new miners and uses. Since Bitcoin's inception, there have been upwards of 2000 altcoins created.

A digital asset is anything that exists in a binary form and comes with the right to use. Cryptocurrency is designed to work as a medium of exchange using cryptography to secure the transactions. To control the creation of additional units, and to verify the transfer of assets, Cryptocurrencies are classified as a subset of digital currencies and are also classified as a subset of alternative currencies and virtual currencies.

Bitcoin and its derivatives use decentralised control as opposed to centralised electronic money/centralised banking systems. The decentralised control is related to the use of bitcoin's blockchain transaction database in the role of a distributed ledger. Decentralised cryptocurrency is produced by the entire cryptocurrency system collectively, at a rate which is pre-defined.

In centralised banking and economic systems such as the Federal Reserve System, corporate boards or governments control the supply of currency by printing units of fiat money or demanding additions to digital banking ledgers.

In the case of decentralised cryptocurrency, companies or governments cannot produce new units.

Within cryptocurrency systems, the safety, integrity, and balance of ledgers are maintained by a community of mutually distrustful parties referred to as miners: members of the general public using their computers to help validate and timestamp transactions adding them to the ledger by a particular timestamping scheme. Miners have a financial incentive to maintain the security of a cryptocurrency ledger.

ASSET OR CURRENCY?

Prior to 2018, cryptocurrencies were primarily considered as currencies just like the Australian or US dollar, British pound or Poland's zloty. This was because the pioneer of cryptocurrency, Bitcoin, was created by Satoshi Nakamoto in 2009 with the aim of replacing the then unstable and centralized fiat currencies.

In the course of 2018, cryptocurrencies experienced a sharp decline following unprecedented volatilities such as government regulation, widespread fraud, and security breaches. Organizations such as UNCTAD, The World Bank, the US Securities and Exchange Commission (SEC), India's Reserve Bank, the G20, and many others then stepped in and asserted that cryptos are assets. However, crypto developers refute this proposition, as they are certain that cryptos are currencies.

Cryptos Are Created to Be Currencies
The whole concept was inspired by the 2008/09 financial crisis that started with the collapse of Lehman Brothers. Afterward, fears gripped the markets that banks and financial institutions had issued loans without assessing the creditworthiness of the borrowers or investment risks that those loans were intended to finance. One of the areas was mortgage and home loan refinancing.

There were a sharp credit crunch and widespread public mistrust of governments, banks and financial institutions that failed to live up to their commitment to protecting deposits.

From the conceptualization of Bitcoin, other cryptos such as Ethereum (ETH), Ripple (XRP), Monero, Dash, Cardano, Litecoin, etc. were developed. Their parent blockchain platforms have crypto wallet features that allow users to transfer their cryptos to their peers in exchange for goods and services. Additionally, the crypto wallets act as a point of deposit for on-platform activities such as mining or others. These wallets act like bank accounts. The transfer feature gives cryptos the ability to substitute fiat currencies.

What is the Threshold for Currency Determination?

For a commodity to be accepted as a currency, there is a threshold of factors that have to be met. The first one is sovereignty. This means that a state has to issue a legal tender and be able to exercise legal power over it. Cryptos fall short of this threshold, as they are decentralized in nature and global for that matter. This is the main logic that bodies such as the Bank of England, the World Bank, etc. have stated categorically that they are assets.

The second aspect is acceptability. Money has to be acceptable to merchants in an economy to be a currency. Crypto acceptance is not universal. A study by the Bank of the Netherlands states that only 2% of online transactions are crypto-based. Based on this assumption, it is clear that cryptos are more of an asset than currency.

Thirdly, money is a unit of account and has to have divisibility to account for all changes in transactions. Cryptos can be a unit of account, and they are divisible to smaller units like other fiat monies.

Lastly, the supply of money has to be determined by monetary policies to influence economic momentum. Cryptos supply is stable and irreversible, unlike fiat money that can be printed at any time, with or without backing. This aspect makes cryptos more of an asset than a currency.

Cryptos are more of assets than currencies

The conclusion from the comparisons is that cryptos are digital assets rather than currencies. However, this can change if there is a surge in public trust when cryptos stabilize against volatilities and governments accept them. Until then, they remain to be assets as the key motive for purchasing cryptos is primarily speculative rather than transactive.

BITCOIN

Bitcoin was created in 2009 by an individual or a group using the pseudonym Satoshi Nakamoto. It is a digital payment system based on mathematical calculations as proof to create a means of exchange that is decentralised and can be secure, verifiable and immutably transferred electronically.

Bitcoin is a cryptocurrency as well as a worldwide payment system. This system can be split into two components. These are bitcoin-the-token and bitcoin-the-protocol. Both are commonly referred to as bitcoin, but the protocol maintains the ledger of balances of the token.

Value as a currency
Bitcoin was the first cryptocurrency created. Its value since 2009 when it was released has been increasing. It even managed to reach an all-time high of USD$17,900 for one bitcoin.

How to get and own bitcoins
To own bitcoins, you must have a digital wallet. This wallet is 'similar' to your physical wallet, as you put bitcoins in and can use them from there, just like a virtual bank account. This wallet exists on your computer or in the cloud.

To acquire bitcoins, you can purchase them from vendors using fiat currency and add them to your digital wallet. Such vendors can be found in digital marketplaces called 'bitcoin exchanges'. A few popular exchanges include Coinbase and Bitstamp. These exchanges allow buyers to trade different currencies from their traditional banking institutions for bitcoins.

Alternatively, if you cannot buy bitcoins, you can mine them. Your computer, or 'miner', solves complex mathematical puzzles, and in return for successfully solving them, you get rewarded bitcoins.

Why Bitcoin?
Bitcoin offers many advantages. Besides being used to make purchases online anonymously, they can be used to conduct international payments and money transfers that are cheap, decentralised and beyond the control of governments or corrupt bodies. Small business owners also benefit from this system as they do not have to pay credit card fees on transactions. And finally, some people see bitcoin as an investment opportunity since the price of bitcoin has been on the rise.

How bitcoin differs from customary currencies
The most important feature of bitcoins is that they are a decentralised system of currency. No institution (government, private, etc.) controls the bitcoin system. Volunteer coders do the maintenance.

There is a limited supply of bitcoins. Fiat currencies that are being used currently have a limitless supply, as central banks can issue as much as they need to. Supply of bitcoin is regulated tightly by an underlying algorithm that limits total bitcoin ever released to 21 million.
As a result of this limit, a very small number of bitcoins are released through mining every hour. This makes bitcoin an attractive asset for investors, as the demand will grow and the supply will be constant.

Within the bitcoin system, there is immutability as transactions once verified cannot be reversed. Because there is no regulator to oversee transactions, they cannot be cancelled.

There is divisibility with this system as the smallest unit is called a Satoshi and is only 0.00000001 bitcoins – one millionth.

BLOCKCHAIN

The blockchain is the brainchild of a person or group of people known by the pseudonym Satoshi Nakamoto. By allowing digital information to be distributed but not copied, blockchain technology created the backbone of a new type of Internet. Originally devised for the digital currency bitcoin, the tech community is now finding other potential uses for the technology. Today, the blockchain is expanding rapidly across many industries on a global scale.

Bitcoin has been called 'digital gold,' and for good reason. To date, the total value of the currency is close to $130 billion US. And blockchains can make other types of digital value. Like the Internet (medical records, advertising), you don't need to know how the blockchain works to use it. However, having a basic knowledge of this new technology shows why it's considered revolutionary.

With a blockchain, many people can write entries into a record of information, and a community of users can control how the record of information is amended and updated. No one person controls the information.

The distributed database created by blockchain technology has a fundamentally different digital backbone. This is also the most distinct and important feature of blockchain technology.

In the case of a blockchain, every node in the network is coming to the same conclusion, each updating the record independently, with the most popular record becoming the de-facto official record instead of there being a master copy.

The blockchain will change the way people and businesses trust. Because of the decentralised method of storing information, the blockchain ledger cannot be tampered with. It is this difference that makes blockchain technology so useful. It represents an innovation in information registration and distribution that eliminates the need for a trusted party to facilitate digital relationships.

Blockchain technology, for all its merits, is not a new technology. It is a combination of already proven technologies that have been applied in a new way. It was the particular orchestration of three technologies (the Internet, private key cryptography and a protocol governing incentivisation) that made bitcoin creator Satoshi Nakamoto's idea so useful.

Trust is a risk judgment between different parties, and in the digital world, determining trust often boils down to proving identity (authentication) and proving permissions (authorisation).

Put in simple terms, we want to confirm, 'Are you who you say you are?' and 'Should you be able to do what you are trying to do?'

In the case of blockchain technology, private key cryptography provides a powerful ownership tool that fulfils authentication requirements. Possession of a private key is ownership. It also spares a person from having to share more personal information than they would need to for an exchange, leaving them exposed to hackers.

This distributed network must also be committed to the transaction network's recordkeeping and security. Authorising transactions is a result of the entire network applying the rules upon which it was designed (the blockchain's protocol).

In fact, the idea that cryptographic keys and shared ledgers can incentivise users to secure and formalise digital relationships has imaginations running wild, with the potential for the blockchains use in almost any field. From governments to IT firms to banks – everyone is seeking to build this additional transaction layer.

Authentication and authorisation, vital to digital transactions, are established as a result of the configuration of blockchain technology. The idea can be applied to any need for a trustworthy system of record.

DAO

DECENTRALISED AUTONOMOUS ORGANISATION

You will often notice that you have to deal with a lot of restrictions whenever you want to complete a business transaction. You cannot work on your own rules, and you need to follow the guidelines given by local authorities and even use the financial services offered by institutions that are approved by the government. However, decentralized autonomous organizations provide a completely flexible platform for people to conduct different transactions online in a secure manner. The future of this platform looks very good as more and more investors and individuals are able to conduct business without any restrictions.

Works on smart contracts
This is similar to the agreement that you make in the traditional world, and you can include various terms and conditions according to the nature of your business. The biggest advantage of using smart contracts is that this offers complete flexibility with regards to setting the terms and you can negotiate them with the other party and include them in the form of computer code.

When the required criteria for the code is met, it automatically gets executed and the transaction is completed. This reduces human intervention by a huge margin and makes it very convenient for users to get into contracts with different individuals and companies across the world.

Contract may not be legal
This is one important thing you have to understand about decentralized autonomous organizations and be very careful of when you are dealing in financial transactions. Remember that decentralized autonomous organizations are not legal entities and the smart contract deployed via computer code may not be valid in legal terms.

However, you can include the terms after taking legal suggestions, and this can protect the transaction to a large extent. In this regard, it makes sense to consult a professional legal representative before you get involved in a smart contract on a blockchain.

Risks involved with DAO

Smart contracts are computer codes written by individuals, and they can contain loopholes that can be exploited by different hackers. These can completely destroy an entire network as people will lose confidence in such a platform when an attack happens to the smart contracts.

In this situation, you may not get enough protection from legal authorities as smart contracts may not be completely valid in proper legal terms. Understanding the risks associated with such platforms will enable you to deal with them in a proper manner.

DAPP

DECENTRALISED APPLICATION

A decentralized application is also referred to as dapp, DAPP, Dapp, dApp or Dapp (pronounced dee-app). As a simple definition, it is an application that runs on a decentralized network. Decentralized applications run on peer-to-peer networks (P2P) rather than a single computer and are not deployed by any single individual or company. These applications have been designed to function on the Internet in a manner that prevents any single entity from controlling them. This has been made possible by blockchain, which is key in the development of the decentralized applications, although they do not necessarily need to run on the blockchain. Such examples are Tor, torrents, and other traditional P2P apps running on a P2P network. dApps can also have an unlimited number of participants on either side of the market.

Reasons for development of decentralized applications
Internet users do not have autonomous control over the information that they share on many websites today. However, Ethereum attempts to correct this flaw in the Internet design using blockchain technology. It is made like an app store that is decentralized, unlike many of today's app stores. Anyone can publish their dApp, which would then be unstoppable. There is no need for a middleman to function efficiently and manage user's data.

Blockchain dApps
In blockchain, an application can only be considered as decentralized if it meets the following requirements:
1) The storage of data of the application must be done cryptographically, in a public and decentralized blockchain. This is done in order to evade any principal points of failure.
2) The entire application must be completely open-source. Its operation must be autonomous, and there should be no entity controlling the bulk of the tokens. The consensus of its users must decide any changes, although it may adapt its protocol in reaction to suggested improvements and feedback.

3) The application should use a cryptographic token.
4) The application must be able to generate tokens.

Types and development of dApps

There are 3 types of dApps, classified according to several characteristics. The classification here is based on whether they use the blockchain of another dApp or they have their own blockchain. This gives us three types:

1) The first type is those that have their own blockchain for example bitcoin.

2) The second type uses the blockchain of the first type. Type 2 dApps have their own protocol, and also the necessary tokens for functioning. An example is the Omni Protocol application.

3) The third type uses the protocol of the second type dApps. They also have the necessary tokens for their functioning. An example is the SAFE Network, which uses Omni Protocol.

In their development, there are three steps that must be satisfied. The first step is publishing a whitepaper describing the dApp itself and its features. After the release of this paper, the feedback from the community is essential in developing the application. The second step involves the distribution of initial tokens. In the final step, the ownership stake of the dApp is then spread. If all three steps are fulfilled, then you have yourself a decentralized application.

DECENTRALISATION

What is decentralisation?
In the 2008/09 financial crisis, most of the global financial systems especially in North America and Western Europe were devastated. The problem started with the collapse of Lehman Brothers Group and spread market fears leading to panic, credit crash, and consequential property market bubble burst. The general effect was lack of trust in institutions and a growing quest for independence from reliance on centralized authorities.

The concept of decentralisation was conceived in the Bitcoin presentation of a new blockchain model. It means the elimination of third parties such as banks, investment firms, etc., and facilitation of peer-to-peer transaction within a network. In other words, the lack of a centralised center of command ensures that end users interact directly. Hence, in a decentralised blockchain, the users manage their transactions directly, and there is no involvement of third parties.

How does decentralisation work?
A blockchain is a distributed ledger technology (DLT) network. The decentralised nature means that the network peers are in charge of utilising the network and making the ecosystem function as it was intended.

With the absence of a central authority to guide interactions, there is a consensus protocol to ensure that peers transact with each other in deals that are not only acceptable to each party but also in line with the ecosystem's requirement.

A Blockchain is built on a consensus protocol that enhances decentralisation. It is a set of rules that govern a network and describes the way in which transmission of data and communication between electronic nodes on a DLT and on-platform features works. The in-built mechanisms, therefore, eliminates the need for third parties to authenticate and record transactions. Summarily, the consensus protocol ensures that all on-platform activities achieve "consensus."

Additionally, most decentralised blockchains have a utility token. They can be acquired either through an ICO sale, Crypto exchange market or on-platform activities between peers. The tokens are a symbol of value and a proof or work indicator that peers are awarded or pay after a transaction. They facilitate decentralization by acting as a unit of value in the absence of fiat currencies.

What are the benefits of decentralisation?

The benefits of decentralisation in blockchain far outweigh the challenges that are present such as, risks, lack of trust, or tax avoidance. The benefits are:

Affordable transactions - The lack of intermediaries means that network users are not tasked with funding the cost of operations to the third parties. Therefore, the fees that are charged either go towards a common fund to improve the blockchain, towards peers or are simply not applicable at all.

Secure transactions - Hackers can breach centralised systems since there is only one focal point to target unlike in a decentralised DLT where there are endless nodes that contains only a negligible fraction of the network's data.

Transparent interactions - Peer-to-peer transactions guarantee transparency on the distributed ledgers eliminating corruption or dubious transactions.

Privacy enhancing - Users can encrypt their identity to ensure that their identity is not identifiable to third parties.

Globalisation facilitation - Decentralisation of networks ensure that anyone can participate in the network activities depending on the whitelist. This aspect is critical for global payment systems, global exchange of ideas, etc.

DISTRIBUTED LEDGER

A ledger generally refers to a book or any collection of financial transactions and accounts. This is the groundwork in accounting and is as old as money and writing. Ledgers have been at the heart of commerce since ancient times and have been used to keep records of many things, although more popularly to record property and money.

The distributed ledger technology (DLT)
A distributed ledger or shared ledger is an asset database which can be shared across a network of multiple sites, geographies and institutions. This technology uses independent computers to share, record and synchronise transactions in their electronic ledgers and exists as a record which is updated and held by every person in a cryptocurrency network. This ledger's distribution is not from a central point. It is unique in that it is created independently by every node (person) and held by them. If there is agreement, then the ledger is updated. All nodes will retain their own copies of the DLT, which are identical.

This design permits a unique ability, making this a record keeping system that is more than a simple database.

The blockchain is one of the types of the distributed ledger. A combination of blockchain and DLT form the building blocks of 'Internet value' and enable recording interactions and transferring 'value' from peer-to-peer, without the requirement of a central entity. This is the primary building block for cryptocurrencies and their values.

Types of distributed ledger technology
DLTs may be permissionless or permissioned, depending on whether anyone or just the approved persons can run a node to validate transactions. They also vary depending on the consensus algorithm (proof of stake, proof of work, or voting systems). Another classification is whether they are mineable or not.

Security of the system

Accuracy and security of this ledger system are maintained cryptographically. This is done through the use of signatures and 'keys' to control what a specific person can do to the ledger. The updating of the ledger depends on the type, as it can be done selectively by one, some or all participants.

Uses of the distributed ledger

In cryptocurrency, the distributed ledger created is permissionless so that anyone can update it. It is possible for anyone to add a block of transactions, but only after being able to solve a complex cryptographic puzzle to allow them to add it. This is what we refer to as mining in cryptocurrency, as after doing this one gets rewarded with the cryptocurrency.

This ledger system, however, can be applied in many other fields. These may include but are not limited to the collection of taxes, issuance of passports, recording land entries, assuring the supply chain of goods and delivering benefits. The applications of this technology appear to be limitless.

DOUBLE SPENDING

Bitcoin and other cryptocurrencies do not have any physical form; they are digital files that can be duplicated. In the cryptocurrency domain, people can manipulate their way to pay more than once with a bitcoin – this is double-spending.

Let's say Alice has only one Bitcoin in her wallet, and she decides to send it to Bob; we call this 'transaction 1'. Now this transaction will go into the unconfirmed transaction pool where it will wait to be cleared.

Meanwhile, Alice sends the same bitcoin to Chris; we call this 'transaction 2'. This will also go in unconfirmed transaction pool and will wait for clearance.

Alice has only one bitcoin in her wallet that she has now sent to both Bob and Chris; we have a double spending problem.

When transactions are pulled out of the unconfirmed transaction pool, they are checked for validity by miners before placing them on the digital ledger. So when transaction 1 is pulled out of the unconfirmed transaction pool, it will be validated since Alice has 1 bitcoin in her wallet. Next, when transaction 2 is pulled out of the unconfirmed transaction pool, it is rejected as Alice does not have any remaining bitcoin in her wallet.

But what if both transaction 1 and 2 are pulled out simultaneously from the unconfirmed transaction pool. In that case, both transactions are valid as they both have necessary funds in their wallet. To sort out that issue we have two branches of the blockchain, and a race will begin, the one who wins the next block will win the race and will place the transaction in the blockchain. If both these branches reach the next block simultaneously, then another race will happen and so on.

This is why it is recommended to wait for six confirmations before considering a transaction complete. Here, 6 confirmations simply mean that after a transaction was added to the blockchain, 6 more

blocks containing several other transactions were added after it.
In the end, we will have only one clear winner, and only one transaction will be confirmed.

Blockchain uses the concept of Proof-of-Work (PoW) to solve the 'double spending problem' (Bitcoin uses the Hashcash PoW system).

How Double Spending happens:

51% attack
These attacks can occur if a group of miners gets control of more than 50% of the network's mining hashrate (computing power). This will allow the miners to prevent new transactions from getting confirmed, allowing them to stop payments between some or all users. They would also be able to reverse transactions that were completed while they were in control of the network, meaning they could double-spend the coins. 51% attacks are just hypothetical attacks and have never occurred so far.

Race Attack
These types of attack occur when somebody sends two conflicting transactions rapidly into the bitcoin network. Merchants that accept unconfirmed transactions are victims of 'Race Attack'. For instance, two transactions are created from the same fund and are then sent to two different merchants. Only one of those merchants will receive the funds, but the sender will get benefits from both of transactions.
To avoid Race Attacks, always only accept transactions that are confirmed.

ETHEREUM

In simple terms, Ethereum is a platform for using cryptocurrency for various financial transactions across the world. In traditional transactions, different financial transactions are monitored by a centralised agency, and they keep track of all the data with regards to the transactions. However, the Ethereum platform is built to replace such entities. In Ethereum, all the data is stored in a decentralised platform. This has opened the market for different businesses to use cryptocurrency for their financial transactions. Let us get a deeper understanding of the various terms associated with cryptocurrency in order to understand Ethereum properly. The future of this technology looks very promising, and it has the potential to drastically affect the way in which people deal with various transactions.

Smart contract
Whenever someone is conducting a financial transaction, it is very important to have a contract as this provides the appropriate security for the transaction. When using fiat currency, the contract is based on the value of the currency that is backed by the financial Institutions of the country. In a similar way, the smart contract of Ethereum is the computer code that facilitates the financial transaction between different users. The smart contracts run on the blockchain, and this is the biggest advantage of using cryptocurrencies.

There are no restrictions with regards to using the currency, and users are not faced with any interference from third-party agencies. When two individuals decide to enter into a contract, the code is written into the blockchain and the contract is stored in a public ledger. Depending upon the terms mentioned in the code, the contract gets executed and you can also mention an expiry date for the contract. In this way, the privacy of individuals involved in the contract is maintained and there is no risk with losing important data with regards to the transaction.

Present applications of Ethereum
Developers across the world can use this system to deploy decentralised applications for various financial transactions. They are not controlled by any centralised agency or individuals, and this is the main advantage of using such networks. It provides complete security while allowing for convenient completion of financial transactions with different individuals. The risk of hacking is reduced by a huge margin as there is no single server that maintains all the data about the financial transactions. This gives enough confidence to users, and they can conveniently use such cryptocurrencies for business transactions.

Future applications of Ethereum
At the moment, the system is used for various transactions in the financial market and the Insurance sector. Apart from that, some contracts are being exchanged in the real estate sector using the Ethereum platform. This multi-functionality gives investors and traders a flexible option to utilise their assets for funding their business activities.

It is also possible for different individuals to develop apps using the Ethereum network. You can also use the Ethereum browser to develop different decentralised applications for your business activities. You need not worry about having technical knowledge when you choose this platform as it is very easy to build blockchain apps using this technology.

FORKS

A fork is a technical event that occurs when mining cryptocurrencies. There are three types of forks, although the major and widely known are two. A fork occurs on any blockchain when various participants agree on collective rules. It is what transpires after a blockchain has separated into two paths forward. There are two options for it to proceed and there has to be proven support for whichever option is chosen over the other option.

Forks can happen, for instance, when two people mining find a block at a similar time. Since there can be only one block, this is resolved by the addition of other blocks to make the longest one, and the other is ignored by the cryptocurrency network. Here the miner whose block was longest gets the block reward. The other becomes an invalid block and is not rewarded.

Developers can intentionally introduce forks into the network. This happens when they need to modify the rules that the software has been using to validate transactions. In such a case, if one mines a block that contains null and void transactions, this block is disregarded by the network. Therefore, miners will want only to mine blocks that have valid transactions and build the longest chains.

SOFT FORK
What it is
This is a rule change that is backwards compatible. This means that the novel rules are interoperable with the longstanding protocol. For example, instead of blocks sized 1MB, the new rule may only allow 500Kb blocks.

How it works
This backwards compatibility means that the nodes that have not been upgraded yet see novel transactions as valid; however, if they continue mining blocks, they will be precluded by nodes which have upgraded. It is for this reason that soft forks require the bulk of hash power on the network.

If a soft fork is maintained by the minority of hash rate within the network, it may be abandoned by the network. Otherwise, it becomes a hard fork.

HARD FORK
What it is
This is a software upgrade to the cryptocurrency network that introduces a new rule, which is not backwards compatible. This is like an expansion of the rules. For example, a new rule that makes blocks 2MB instead of 1MB.

How it works
Any nodes running the old software will find new transactions as invalid. Therefore, all nodes on the network must upgrade to continue mining valid blocks.

A problem can arise if a portion of the community decides to stick to the old rules. There will arise a political impasse.
The other type of fork is the user activated soft fork.

ICO

INITIAL COIN OFFERING

An ICO (Initial Coin Offering) is the 'crypto' equivalent of launching a start-up – a new service (valued by its digital currency) placed onto the market with a variety of offers promoted for its 'stock' (coins).

ICOs typically come in several forms:

AirDrop
The coin's creators give out free coins to users in the hope they'll start trading them with friends, etc.

Pre-Sale
The most common form of ICO – selling coins before they're released to the public. The idea is that the 'private' valuation of the coin will be less than the public price, giving early adopters the opportunity to make quick profits.

Pre-Mining
When a coin developer allocates some coins to a single address before the coin goes live. This is meant to be compensation for the developer's work, but it can also act as a safety net for maintaining the value of the coins, etc.

How ICOs Make Money
The money-making aspect is not as direct as many people think.

You cannot 'buy' a bunch of new coins/tokens and flip them the next day. It can sometimes take months, or even years, for a new coin to become valuable. It's this long-term view which often ruins many new ICO investors.

To understand the process, you need to appreciate the inherent 'value' of crypto, ICOs, bitcoin, and blockchain...

All 'crypto' coins/tokens are the same – they're built on 'decentralization' technology (typically 'blockchain').

Blockchain is a database which runs across many different 'nodes' (computers) – providing a completely independent way to store and manage data without the need of a central processor. The benefit of this is that you're able to build 'decentralized' applications – such as Bitcoin – totally independent of third-party agents and owned by the users and managed by the community.

What used to be under the remit of a huge data-provider (Facebook, Google, Governments, Banks, etc.) can now be completely managed by the users – allowing for direct ('peer to peer') transactions and custom methods / systems for managing and storing data.

Bitcoin is a decentralized financial ledger – it stores transactions between users in a database that's neither owned nor operated by any single individual. It is not a bank – it's simply the equivalent of a huge set of 'bank accounts'.

The 'value' of a BTC is presently based on its ability to transcend regulatory procedure – because Bitcoin is entirely decentralized, it means that you are able to 'trade' its coins directly with other people. In theory, this means that I'm able to move money out of the reach of governments / banks.

To this end, when you appreciate that Bitcoin is essentially an 'application' that runs across 1,000s of computers, you'll begin to see that ICOs work in very similar ways – they're applications built on top of the blockchain's decentralized database to provide transactional functionality to a range of services, funds and assets.

MINING

The era of cryptocurrency started when Satoshi Nakamoto published his famous 'Bitcoin: A Peer-to-Peer Electronic Cash System' whitepaper. Cryptocurrency was born to be decentralised and distributed.

Since there is no single authority in Bitcoin (BTC) and other cryptocurrencies, how are transactions written over the blockchain managed and how are new crypto tokens generated?

Mining verifies transactions on the blockchain and releases new coins by solving mathematical problems linked to the blockchain.

Miners are computational nodes in the blockchain network that approve Bitcoin and other cryptocurrency transactions. They ensure that every transaction written on the blockchain is legitimate and they do so by spending computational power to verify every transaction. Miners provide stability and integrity to the security of the blockchain network.

All miners on the blockchain network are racing to solve a complex mathematical problem. Whoever solves the problem first will be rewarded the next block in the blockchain. New bitcoins are generated with every new block and are given as an economic incentive to the miners.

Genesis Block
Every blockchain has a genesis block or block 0, i.e., the first block. Every block created after the genesis block is automatically linked back to its ancestor block and the chain goes on until it reaches the genesis block.

Bitcoin's genesis block was established on January 3, 2009, at 18:15:05 GMT. Block header hash of Bitcoin's genesis block is:
000000000019d6689c085ae165831e934ff763ae46a2a6c172b3f-1b60a8ce26f

---

The previous hash has all zeros (which confirms that nothing is before this block) and it was mined using the same hashing algorithm that is used today but with a difficulty level of 1. The reward for mining this block was 50 Bitcoins.

Initially, the reward for mining one Bitcoin block was 50 bitcoins per block, which then halved to 25 per block and right now is around 12.5 per block. The difficulty of the mathematical problem which miners have to solve increases as more miners join the network.

The total number of bitcoins ever to be released is limited to 21 million coins. Based on current estimates, the last bitcoin will be mined by 2140. After that, there will be no bitcoins rewarded to miners for their services.

Mining was possible on PCs and laptops in initial days when the complexity level of the mathematical problem was lower, but very few miners took it seriously at that time. Today, mining is only viable on specialised hardware. Avalon6, AntMiner S7, and AntMiner S9 are some of the mining hardware processors for mining Bitcoin.

OPPORTUNITIES

There are opportunities galore when it comes to the cryptocurrency space, the possibilities are seemingly endless for anyone looking to earn a bit of extra money on the side, or maybe just to expand their knowledge of the subject. The possibilities don't have to be linked to money, but the majority of opportunities that do exist are linked with money. We will go over some of the many opportunities that you can get started with.

#1 – Mining
This is the process of adding new transactions to the blockchain of a cryptocurrency, so adding bitcoin transactions to the Bitcoin blockchain. While mining is largely associated with bitcoin, other cryptocurrencies are also allowing people to mine their cryptos too. This process can be done from a dedicated computer that is specifically built for the sole purpose of mining cryptocurrencies and nothing else. These computing systems require incredibly fast CPUs and powerful GPUs, and because of this, they output a large amount of electricity compared to the computer that you are reading this on. Many altcoin fans have experienced relative success in mining because they aren't as popular or as well-known when comparing them to the likes of bitcoin, ethereum, ripple or dash, etc.

#2 – Trading
Some of the major cryptocurrencies are now featured on the world's financial markets and are available to trade. This means that you can make money on them without actually having to own the cryptocurrency itself, this is because you are only purchasing a futures contract which represents the ownership, not the cryptocurrency itself. All the major trading platforms like IG Index, MT4 and Trading212 all feature the major cryptocurrencies, all with free technical trading tools that you can use to help make more informed decisions as to when you should buy or sell certain cryptos.

#3 – Programming

Might sound like a strange one, but we wouldn't have cryptocurrencies today let alone blockchain technology without programmers. Since all cryptocurrencies are simply lines of computer code that have a certain level of value attached to them, theoretically anyone could create their own virtual currency. But it doesn't stop there because there are marketplaces available that allow people to buy, sell and trade virtual currencies on an open market and these will have had to have been coded and programmed to handle the transactions on the marketplace. The monetary value of some of these exchange platforms is enormous, and the number of transactions that they process is also an insane amount, and some take a fee for processing transactions too!

#4 – Writing

Writing gives everyone the opportunity to learn and advance their knowledge of a specific field. Platforms like Steemit pay people to write high-quality content, and they get paid in cryptocurrency known as 'steem'. The Steemit platform works by attracting writers onto their platform to write an article on anything they want, and if that article is high quality and people like to read it and vote on it, then the author gets paid. It is as simple as that.

The possibilities in the blockchain and cryptocurrency space are endless and the only thing holding people back is their imagination, so if you want to earn a bit of money on the side or expand your knowledge, you know where to start!

PEER-TO-PEER

A peer-to-peer (p2p) connection entails the linking of two or more computers directly. The basic idea is to eliminate a centralized server that serves to moderate the interactions between two computer users who in this context are referred to as peers. The connections enable users to share files or devices such as printers amongst themselves.

What Is It?
A peer-to-peer (p2p) network can occur in three categories. They include the universal serial bus (USB) connections, local area infrastructure connections, and applications such as blockchain software.

A USB is the most basic p2p connection. In this class, a user transfer files to an external USB location that then enables different people to access the file without having to rely on a centralized computer server. Secondly, there is the aspect of a local area infrastructure. This is common in workplaces where the staff work from a localized platform. This type of peer-to-peer interaction is common in banks, insurance firms, universities or even health centers. The staff are network peers and what they update on the site can be seen by everyone with access. In some cases, there could be restrictions or authorized access depending on the seniority or work specialization of a staff.

Thirdly, local area infrastructures can be facilitated by applications. They enable users to designate files on their computers that they would like to share with other software users. Examples of these applications include Acquisition, Morpheus, BearShare, Limewire, and Kazaa.

Lastly, and most importantly, p2p connections are common to cryptocurrencies and blockchain platforms. Blockchain networks are open and distributed ledgers where users can carry out transactions on p2p levels. When a platform user performs a transaction, he/she is awarded tokens as a proof of work or authority depending on the prevailing protocols.

How It Works

The models of peer-to-peer networks are self-explanatory on the contexts of USB sharing, p2p apps, and local area network infrastructure. Meanwhile, the p2p operations on the context of blockchain are complex as they are relatively new having been introduced from 2009 with the launch of Bitcoin.

In a peer-to-peer blockchain network, there are two-end users. On one side, a user builds the ecosystem's blocks. This entails uploading files, or any other file that can the platform is dedicated to providing. Meanwhile, a user on the receiving end can be able to access that file when they browse the network.

How does it relate to cryptocurrency?

Peer to peer interactions for cryptocurrencies occurs within blockchain networks. When users of a platform transact any operation within an ecosystem such as posting a property for sale in a blockchain platform dedicated to real estate, there are tokens that are earned as a proof of work. These tokens or cryptocurrencies are then stored in a hot or cold crypto wallet that is a secure storage for platform keys and digital assets.

From the crypto wallet, the holders are then able to transfer their tokens to their peers in exchange of on-platform products or services. Additionally, the p2p transfer of cryptocurrencies can occur when the owners wish to trade with peers such as in crypto exchanges or point-of-sale shops that accept crypto payments.

PRIVACY COINS

What are Privacy Coins and why is there a need for them?
Financial privacy is a rare and valued commodity. Our every transaction with fiat currency is recorded and analysed by different financial institutes like banks, and there have been cases where these financial institutes have sold that information to third parties, leading to compromise in the financial privacy of users.

Cryptocurrency was born to be anonymous, i.e., there is no concept of physical identity in cryptocurrency. Even the inventor of Bitcoin Satoshi Nakamoto didn't reveal his original physical identity, and nobody knows why he did so. No personal information is exchanged in cryptocurrency transactions. The sender and receiver both remain anonymous in the process of sending and receiving. This anonymous nature of cryptocurrency has its advantages making it ideal to use in areas where crime rates are high.

You will remain anonymous in BTC and Eth as long as nobody knows the public address associated with you. If somebody comes to know your public address, then they can trace all transactions occurring in and out of your address and also the number of coins residing in your address.

For instance, if you know that Bob owns this address 1933phfhK3ZgFQNLGSDXvqCn32k2buXY8a, you can go to the site blockchain.com and type that address in the search bar, and you will see the complete transaction history associated with this address. Your privacy and anonymity are compromised in this case. That's why cryptocurrencies like Bitcoin are associated with addresses as pseudonyms.

The solution – Privacy Coins
Privacy coins are taking anonymity and privacy to the next level by overcoming the shortcomings of the early generation of cryptocurrency. Privacy coins keep you completely anonymous while you are transacting on the network.

Privacy coins do so by hiding the information of the senders and receivers as well as the amount being sent and received.

Today there are many privacy coins. Below is an overview of Monero

Privacy coin.

Monero (XMR)

Created in April 2014, Monero is designed to be private, secure and untraceable, and it is one of the leaders of the privacy movement in cryptocurrency. This movement is concerned with guaranteeing that you can use cryptocurrencies however you want, without fear of having your transactions history tracked or exposed.

Here are some reasons why its ranked as the number one privacy coin.

Untraceable: Monero uses a unique technology called 'ring signatures' which shuffles users' public keys eliminating the possibility of identifying a particular user.

Un-linkable: Being un-traceable doesn't protect a receiver from defining his or her balance through inspecting ingoing messages to the users' public address. Therefore, Monero employs a specific protocol which generates multiple unique one-time addresses that can only be linked by the payment receiver and are incapable of being revealed through blockchain analysis.

Secure: Monero is cryptographically secured. The uniqueness of the algorithm consists of such tremendous computational and electric capabilities that a hacker would not even try to steal your funds. Therefore your wallet is unbreakable.

PROOF-OF-STAKE

What Is Proof of Stake?
Of the many controversies which surround cryptocurrency at any given moment, one of the most well-known is regarding bitcoin's outsized power consumption. On average, it takes about as much energy to sustain the bitcoin network for a year as it does to power the entire nation of Ireland.

The driving factor in bitcoin's power-hungry consumption is its consensus algorithm called proof of work. A proof of work algorithm requires a network of miners who use specialized, energy-intensive computer hardware to guess the number which unlocks a block (and its rewards paid in BTC).

In the race to mine more and more bitcoin, massive mining outfits have appeared in places as far-flung as the plains of Wisconsin to caves in central China. As the difficulty of mining bitcoin rises, so too do the power demands required to mine it, resulting in a veritable arms race between miners.

Taking note of the environmentally destructive process of mining, Sunny King and Scott Nadal introduced the proof of stake consensus algorithm in 2012 as a lightweight, scalable, and secure consensus method.

Consensus Building
To understand proof-of-stake, it's essential to understand the role of consensus in blockchain systems. Blockchains are decentralized ledgers that are maintained by a distributed network of nodes which need to agree by majority consensus about incoming transactions before permanently adding them to the ledger.

Consensus between nodes (or miners in the case of bitcoin and other PoW blockchains) is the critical first security step in blockchain systems that allow them to avoid attacks (double-spending, Byzantine, and others) while staying distributed and trustful.

Building consensus means that the nodes/miners need to validate the transactions by rolling them into a block, agreeing on the block, and then adding it to the history of blocks (thus, blockchain). This is why the main selling point of new blockchain ICOs is the type of consensus algorithm being used. As is often the case, some blockchains opt to run modified versions of proof of work or proof-of-stake systems but, ultimately, they're still using one of the two.

How Proof-of-Stake Works
To build consensus, proof of stake systems do away with miners entirely. Instead of miners, users validate transactions by staking some amount 'X' of the network's token.

Ethereum, the world's second most valuable cryptocurrency by market capitalization, is making the switch from proof-of-work to proof-of-stake sometime in 2019. When they do, achieving consensus on the Ethereum network will look like this:
1. Two users each stake (staking is aking to pledging your tokens for use by the network) an amount of ETH. User 1 stakes 15 ETH and User 2 stakes 115 ETH.

2. The Ethereum network's proof of stake algorithm semi-randomly selects which user will validate the next block of transactions using the age of the staker (how long they have been staking for) and a randomized block selection.

3. If a user fraudulently validates a block by giving the OK to a false transaction, that user is penalised by losing their staked tokens, losing certain rights within the network, or all of the above.

Each proof-of-stake based blockchain can add and subtract modifications to the underlying PoS algorithm as they choose. Regardless of those modifications, proof-of-stake systems put a far lower demand on hardware and electricity, making them much more environmentally friendly and primed to scale to larger transactional volume.

PROOF-OF-WORK

Proof-of-work (PoW) is a consensus algorithm that allows trustless and distributed consensus. It was first used in Bitcoin blockchain and is now the foundation of many open blockchain networks.

The PoW concept existed even before Bitcoin, but Satoshi Nakamoto applied this technique to digital currency.

In the context of cryptocurrency, PoW refers to a computational puzzle that miners (computers in the blockchain network) have to solve, and this allows open blockchain networks to remain secure and decentralised.

PoW uses cryptographic functions that guarantee a certain number of computer cycles were spent to solve the puzzle. In other words, by finding the solution, you are proving that you have spent some time in solving the puzzle hence the term proof-of-work.

Bitcoin uses the Hashcash (how to find the input knowing the output) based proof-of-work system. The problem is hard to solve, but once solved other computers in the network can verify it. The complexity of the puzzle increases as the network grows.

The following analogy helps explain the PoW:

1. Say we have one single person with two dice in his hand. He has to keep on rolling these two dice until the sum appearing on top of both dice equals to 10. He only needs combinations like 5-5, 6-4 and 4-6, since their amount will be equal to 10. To get these combinations, he has to roll both dice again and again as there is little probability that he will get these two combinations in the first attempt.

2. Now to add competition, we add ten more people to this and whoever reaches this combination first wins.

Whoever wins the competition will be given the new block where new transactions are recorded, and the miner will be rewarded economic incentives. This is how open blockchains are secured and managed.

Proof-of-work groups up the transactions and adds them to the block. There is a cost (hardware and electricity) to solve the puzzle.

Limitations of PoW

The main drawback of PoW is that it requires digital calculations which consume lots of electricity and need expensive, specialised hardware (ASIC, GPU).

Although very secure, Proof-of-Work based blockchain networks can be prone to a 51% attack. A 51% attack, or majority attack, is a case where a user or a group of users control the majority of the mining power.

PoW based systems are also slow and have serious performance issues in case of handling a massive number of transactions. Proof-of-Stake (PoS) is an alternate consensus algorithm developed to overcome shortcomings of PoW.

SMART CONTRACTS

Nick Zsabo first raised the subject of smart contracts in 1997. He argued that the 'formalisation of our relationships—especially contracts—provide the blueprint for ideal security'.

Zsabo uses a vending machine to explain the mechanics of a smart contract:
'A canonical real-life example, which we might consider to be the primitive ancestor of smart contracts, is the humble vending machine. Within a limited amount of potential loss (the amount in the till should be less than the cost of breaching the mechanism), the machine takes in coins, and via a simple mechanism, which makes a freshman computer science problem in design with finite automata, dispense change and product according to the displayed price. The vending machine is a contract with bearer: anybody with coins can participate in an exchange with the vendor. The lockbox and other security mechanisms protect the stored coins and contents from attackers, sufficiently to allow profitable deployment of vending machines in a wide variety of areas.'

Smart contracts are an efficient way to help people perform certain tasks. Some of these tasks include being able to exchange money, property, shares or typically anything of value in a stress and conflict free way, all while avoiding the services of intermediaries who add to the total cost for them to profit. If you needed the services of a lawyer for legal documents, then you would approach the lawyer (intermediary) and pay them and then wait to receive those documents. However, when it comes to smart contracts, all you need to do is insert a cryptocurrency like bitcoin into the virtual vending machine, and out pops your legal document or whatever it is you require. Smart contracts are becoming more and more frequent in the professional world, due to their functionality and their scalability, not only do smart contracts define the rules and the penalties surrounding an agreement the same way as a traditional agreement, but they can automatically enforce those obligations.

An example of how smart contracts can operate professionally is through paying rent. Imagine you are renting a property from someone and there is an option to pay the rent in cryptocurrency through the use of the blockchain. On the date that the rent is due to be paid, you will receive a digital entry key, which should arrive on a specified date; however, if it doesn't arrive on time, then a refund is processed by the blockchain. On the other hand, if the digital key is released to you before the specified date, the built-in function within the smart contracts holds it until the specified date, to which you would pay the rent to the owner. Smart contracts work on an if-then basis, so you can expect these contracts to work with few risks of error.

STABLE COINS

What are Stable Coins?
Cryptocurrency markets are notoriously volatile. Much like rough seas, crypto markets swing up and down, with rare sideways moments of calm. Apart from inhospitable trading conditions, market volatility also creates liquidity problems for traders and investors alike.

The question put to crypto traders is this: With digital asset prices swinging wildly, how does one escape from a trade intact without going back to fiat currency? Apart from tax implications that arise from trading back to AUD, USD, EUR or any other government-issued currency, there are limited trading pair options for fiat to crypto at most exchanges.

Cryptocurrency and the blockchain tech which underpins it is a new, innovative asset class that requires new, innovative solutions to liquidity problems. As such, stable coins were invented as intermediary tokens wedged between fiat currency and cryptocurrency for the purpose of creating a safe haven of stability for traders and investors.

How Stable Coins Work
Essentially, stable coins are cryptocurrency assets that are pegged to another stable asset such as USD. Contrary to popular belief, stable coins don't need to be pegged to fiat currency. Instead, stable coins can attach to any stable asset, whether it's gold, silver, or even stable mutual funds.

Crypto's most well known stable coin is Tether (USDT). Tether is backed 1Q1 by USD reserves but has come under plenty of fire in the last year due to a lack of transparency on the part of the Tether foundation.

The controversy surrounding Tether may have led to the sudden rise in stable coin efforts in the last year. Pax, Basis, Sagacoin, Terra, Dai, and are some of the notable efforts, but many more exist.

How To Use Stable Coins

Stable coins are used as a respite from the turbulence of cryptocurrency markets. To imagine what this type of functionality looks like, think of one of bitcoin's typical wild swings within a 3-day time frame.

At the beginning of the time frame in question, bitcoin is sitting at a $6900 price point. On day two, bitcoin's trading volume begins drying up. The price begins to seem anemic with a slow decline starting to form. The day closes at $6750. On day three, with volume continuing to fall, you, the trader, see dramatic downside on the way.

Using Tether (USDT), a stable coin that is pegged to the value of the US Dollar, you sell your BTC on the BTCUSDT trading pair, just catching BTC at $6735. With your USDT balance now sitting at $6735 after selling 1 BTC, the BTC market tanks, and several days later you feel fortuitous after seeing prices drop to $6200.

When you hear traders speak of being Tethered, this is precisely what they mean. Being Tethered is a lot like being tied to a post in a hurricane: the storm rages, but after it passes, you're intact and in the same place, to boot.

In theory, stable coins allow for more money to enter the cryptocurrency market without worry, leading many insiders to speculate that the proliferation of stable coins is a bullish signal for the space in general. Whether that turns out to the case is yet to be seen, but with blockchain technology yet to mature, stable coins are sure to play a significant role.

TRUST

Trust is the ability of individuals to believe that their expectations will be met as per the standards that govern the parties that they are dealing with. In most circumstances, people do not trust each other without a prior acquaintance or experience. Further, because of a high risk, there is usually a need for a third party to impose sanctions when one party breaks the rules that bind them in trust.

In this perspective, trust in the context of blockchain technology refers to the ability of the blockchain network to apply consensus protocols that validate transactions and communications to guarantee that the peer-to-peer interactions are honest, valid and meets the expectation of each user.

How does blockchain eliminate the need for trust in a third party?
As a decentralized platform, a blockchain platform has mechanisms that facilitate trust. They are smart contracts and consensus protocols. Smart contracts, also known as crypto contracts, are blockchain features that directly govern the transfer of assets or digital currencies between peers. They not only ensure that users adhere to the rules and standards but they also ensure that penalties are imposed on users who engage in unfair deals. They generally epitomize the conventional contracts.

Meanwhile, smart contracts work with consensus protocols in a blockchain to ensure that there is an acceptable system of agreement between the transactions among peers and the smart contracts. The two aspects basically create a platform of trust. This eliminates the need for a third party as the interaction on the peer-to-peer transactions are already guaranteed to be fair, acceptable and meeting the expectations.

The elimination of the need to trust a third party by blockchain constitutes a redefinition of trust. Trust concept is being rewritten from the traditional involvement of a human authority to a more modern way of placing trust in a blockchain platform. It becomes easier to trust the system knowing that it is built upon smart contracts, decentralization, and consensus protocol that third parties cannot be trusted to offer.

What does that mean for industries based on being that third party? The redefinition of trust from human controlled (centralized) third parties does not, however, indicate the beginning of the end of third-party institutions such as banks, e-commerce shops like Alibaba and Amazon, or any other third-party industry that is being disrupted. It is an indication that the notion of trust is not appealing to the public when a third party still operates in the conventional system of centralized LAN networks. This is because consumers are starting to trust blockchain technology and all firms should shift to the new platform. Hence, industries should be more innovative and create trust through incorporating blockchain into some of their departments.

What are the benefits to the general population?
Trust is an impetus to the participation of people in a project or a business. Therefore, the way that blockchain is enhancing trust will be vital to the following;

Global economy - people will engage with each other in cross-border transactions and boost economies around the world.

Curbing fraud - when firms realize the importance of trust, they will input mechanisms to protect the interest of users in on-platform activities, this will eliminate fraud and curb cyber-crime that targets individuals.

Trust will reorganize the world and make it more efficient - firms will find it necessary to do away with industry bottlenecks and red tapes. As a consequence, there will be widespread efficiency in basic services and goods production.

USING CRYPTO

The big question around crypto is what can you actually do with cryptocurrencies today, and how can you use cryptocurrencies in day to day life? To some, this is one of life's many unanswered questions because cryptocurrencies aren't like traditional currencies, in the sense that you can physically touch them. However, the fact is, you CAN use cryptocurrencies for many different things. People just don't actually know what they can do with them, so we will go over some of the things that cryptocurrencies can be used for.

#1 – Purchase Goods and Services
The most obvious thing you can do with cryptocurrencies is buy something with it, like goods and services. There are more and more companies who are expanding the way they do business by allowing customers to pay for their goods and services through a varying number of cryptocurrencies like bitcoin, ethereum, ripple or dash. Companies like Microsoft allow you to purchase and download games using bitcoin, and Expedia allows you to book a holiday using cryptocurrency.

#2 – Invest in Start-ups
There are several ways in which an ordinary person can invest in a start-up, whether that be from crowdsourcing websites, or whether they take part in an Initial Coin Offering. An initial coin offering, or ICO, is much like an IPO where funds are raised for a company in exchange for shares that represent ownership. But instead of fiat currencies being used to raise funds, it is actually cryptocurrencies that are being used. The investor will read the documentation which is called a whitepaper released by the company raising funds, and then he or she will follow the proper channels to exchange their cryptos for tokens that represent shares in the start-up. ICOs have become incredibly popular because they are a much easier way of raising funds due to much fewer regulations that are normally enforced when conducting IPOs.

#3 – Send Cryptocurrency to Friends and Family
Once you obtain some cryptocurrency, you have the freedom to do pretty much whatever you want with it, that includes both of the above. You can also initiate transactions and send cryptocurrencies to friends or family as a gift, or maybe because you're feeling generous. What's more is that the process is very simple, almost instantaneous, and doesn't require a third party to handle the transaction for you.

The uses for cryptocurrencies are constantly growing, which means that the popularity for them will increase too and soon you will be able to pay for your groceries or maybe even pay your rent using cryptocurrencies. The rapid expansion of cryptocurrencies and their technologies are becoming part of our society and economy, and soon you might even receive your salary in bitcoin or ethereum. The point is, whether we like it or not they have made themselves known and they seem to be here to stay for the foreseeable future.

WALLETS

A cryptocurrency wallet is a secure digital wallet used to store, send, and receive digital currency like Bitcoin. Most coins have an official wallet or a few officially recommended third-party wallets. To use any cryptocurrency, you will need to use a cryptocurrency wallet.

Cryptocurrency itself is not actually 'stored' in a wallet. Instead, a private key (secure digital code known only to you and your wallet) is stored that shows ownership of a public key (a public digital code connected to a certain amount of currency). Therefore, your wallet stores your private and public keys, allows you to send and receive coins and also acts as a personal ledger of transactions.

Cryptocurrency wallets are all built to be secure, but the exact security differs from wallet to wallet. Generally, like your usernames and passwords, the security of your wallet comes from you using best practices.

Here is a quick breakdown of the different types of cryptocurrency wallets:

Desktop Wallet: The most common type of wallet. Typically an app that connects directly to a coin's client.

Mobile Wallet: A wallet that is run from a smartphone app.

Online Wallet: An online wallet is a web-based wallet. You don't download an app; data is hosted on a real or virtual server. Some online wallets are hybrid wallets allowing encryption of private data before being sent to the online server.

Hardware Wallet: Dedicated hardware built to hold cryptocurrency and keep it secure. This includes USB devices. These devices can go online to make transactions and get data and then can be taken offline for transportation and security.

Paper Wallet: You can print out a QR code for both a public and private key. This allows you to send and receive digital currency using a paper wallet. With this option, you can avoid storing digital data about your currency by using a paper wallet.

The term 'hot wallet' describes a wallet connected to the Internet. The term 'cold wallet' describes a wallet not connected to the Internet.

Get your T-shirt
VISIT:
www.bitcoinbasix.com

FOR MORE RESOURCES VISIT:
www.bitcoinbasix.com